RADICAL
Generosity

RADICAL
Generosity

Living Right *and* Loving Others
in the Name of Jesus

MARVIN WILLIAMS

Discovery House.
from Our Daily Bread Ministries

Radical Generosity: Living Right and Loving Others in the Name of Jesus
© 2016 by Our Daily Bread Ministries

All rights reserved.

Discovery House is affiliated with Our Daily Bread Ministries,
Grand Rapids, Michigan.

Requests for permission to quote from this book should be directed to:
Permissions Department, Discovery House,
P.O. Box 3566, Grand Rapids, MI 49501,
or contact us by e-mail at permissionsdept@dhp.org.

Unless otherwise indicated, Scripture quotations are taken
from The Holy Bible, *New International Version*®, *NIV*®.
Copyright © 1973, 1978, 1984, 2011 by Biblica, Inc.®
Used by permission. All rights reserved worldwide.

Interior design by Beth Shagene

ISBN 978-1-62707-537-4

Printed in the United States of America

First printing in 2016

CONTENTS

INTRODUCTION

On a recent trip to Israel, I was struck by two images. The first image was the Jordan River. The Jordan is the longest and most important river of Palestine. It rises from the foot of Mount Hermon and is a free-flowing tributary that generously channels the blessings of fresh water downstream into many bodies of water, including the Sea of Galilee and the Dead Sea—the second image by which I was struck.

The Dead Sea is beautiful but strangely eerie. This is the case because the Dead Sea is dead. The high salt content makes for a harsh environment in which animals cannot live (hence the name). Though the Jordan River is constantly blessing the Dead Sea with fresh water, the Dead Sea has no outlet to bless other bodies of water.

These two images started me thinking about several

questions regarding my level of generosity. Am I like the Jordan River, channeling God's blessings downstream into the lives of others in need? Am I a free-flowing tributary of God's love and grace? Or am I more like the Dead Sea, allowing the salinity of selfishness to prevent any form of generosity—kindness, compassion, and justice—to flow out to others?

My hope is that the words in this book will challenge and encourage us, individually and collectively, to be more like the Jordan River than the Dead Sea. In a world where people are radically selfish, we, as followers of Jesus, are called to be radically philanthropic, channeling God's blessings downstream into the lives of others. We should live this way because Jesus has been radically generous to us. He left the riches of heaven, became poor, and gave away His life so we could receive life and enjoy a relationship with our heavenly Father.

How should we respond to the generosity of Christ, who gave it all away for our sake? We respond by living lives of intentional gratitude and radical generosity.

—MARVIN WILLIAMS

RADICAL
Generosity

Command those who are rich in this present world not to be arrogant nor to put their hope in wealth, which is so uncertain, but to put their hope in God, who richly provides us with everything for our enjoyment. Command them to do good, to be rich in good deeds, and to be generous and willing to share. In this way they will lay up treasure for themselves as a firm foundation for the coming age, so that they may take hold of the life that is truly life.

1 TIMOTHY 6:17–19

Cindy Kienow, a server at a popular restaurant in Hutchinson, Kansas, had been waiting on one of her steady customers for three years. He always tipped her well, sometimes leaving as much as half the tab. Then he outdid himself—he gave her a $10,000 tip for a $26 meal. He told her, "I want you to know this is not a joke."

What an amazing display of radical generosity!

Paul advised Timothy to encourage the wealthy in his congregation to display radical generosity (1 Timothy 6:18). Timothy ministered in the prosperous city of Ephesus, where certain members of the church were wealthy. Some of these people didn't understand their responsibility to the kingdom of God. So Paul challenged Timothy to remind them that having great wealth carried great responsibility. That included being humble, finding their security in God, not in riches, and using their money to do good for others. How they handled their money revealed the condition of their heart.

Even if we're not wealthy, God has called us to radical generosity. We can share what we do have and be rich in good deeds. If we have a generous attitude about money, we are much more likely to be generous in other matters concerning the Lord's people and His work.

———

WHEN WE GIVE OURSELVES TO THE LORD,
ALL OTHER GIVING BECOMES EASIER.

"You have heard that it was said to the people long ago, 'You shall not murder, and anyone who murders will be subject to judgment.' But I tell you that anyone who is angry with a brother or sister will be subject to judgment. Again, anyone who says to a brother or sister, 'Raca,' is answerable to the court. And anyone who says, 'You fool!' will be in danger of the fire of hell.

"Therefore, if you are offering your gift at the altar and there remember that your brother or sister has something against you, leave your gift there in front of the altar. First go and be reconciled to them; then come and offer your gift.

"Settle matters quickly with your adversary who is taking you to court. Do it while you are still together on the way, or your adversary may hand you over to the judge, and the judge may hand you over to the officer, and you may be thrown into prison. Truly I tell you, you will not get out until you have paid the last penny."

MATTHEW 5:21–26

Several years ago while having lunch with a friend, a white man called me "boy." Shock gave way to anger and hurt. My friend even shed tears. Why? The term *boy* was an insulting label used of black men in the US during slavery—an attempt to steal their identity by demoting them to less than men. As that ugly word recklessly barreled its way through my soul, I wanted to respond with an equally unkind name. But some ancient words from our Master about murder and anger changed my mind.

As Jesus was teaching His followers, He quoted the sixth commandment—"You shall not murder"—and the penalty for breaking it (Matthew 5:21). Then He gave a fuller interpretation. Taking someone's life was not limited to physical murder; you could show contempt for someone through name-calling and be just as guilty. In Jewish culture, to call someone "Raca" or "Fool" (v. 22) was the equivalent of calling someone empty-headed or an idiot. It was a word used to demean and demote another while robbing him of his true identity. What makes name-calling so damaging is that it insults the God who created that person in His image!

Jesus taught His followers that the weight of our neighbor's glory is a burden we carry daily. If we follow His teaching, we won't be guilty of identity theft.

———

TO INSULT THE CREATURE
IS TO INSULT THE CREATOR.

*Paul and his companions traveled throughout the region
of Phrygia and Galatia, having been kept by the Holy Spirit
from preaching the word in the province of Asia. When they
came to the border of Mysia, they tried to enter Bithynia, but
the Spirit of Jesus would not allow them to. So they passed
by Mysia and went down to Troas. During the night Paul
had a vision of a man of Macedonia standing and begging
him, "Come over to Macedonia and help us." After Paul had
seen the vision, we got ready at once to leave for Macedonia,
concluding that God had called us to preach the gospel to them.*

ACTS 16:6–10

One Friday, my day of rest as a pastor, the Holy Spirit prompted me to call a young single mother in our faith community to see if her car had been repaired. I had some reservations about making the call, but I obeyed.

Little did I know that my obedience would help save her life! She said later: "Friday at work I was planning on taking my life, but in a time of need, I believe God was there for me. He had Pastor Williams call me, and just by listening to his voice, let me know that God loved me."

The apostle Paul must have had a few reservations of his own when the Holy Spirit prompted him and his team not to go into the provinces of Asia and Bithynia. Instead, they felt the Spirit's call to go into Macedonia to preach the good news. In each situation, they obeyed the Spirit's promptings. As a result, Paul and his team were instrumental in giving birth to a new faith community in Philippi (Acts 16:11–15).

As believers in Christ who are indwelt by the Holy Spirit, our desire should be to please Him. May we not grieve the Holy Spirit by ignoring His gentle promptings. When we obey Him, we might be used by God to lead someone to Christ, to disciple new believers—or even to help save somebody's life.

———

MAKE THE RIGHT CHOICE:
OBEY THE SPIRIT'S VOICE.

Someone in the crowd said to [Jesus], "Teacher, tell my brother to divide the inheritance with me."

Jesus replied, "Man, who appointed me a judge or an arbiter between you?" Then he said to them, "Watch out! Be on your guard against all kinds of greed; life does not consist in an abundance of possessions."

And he told them this parable: "The ground of a certain rich man yielded an abundant harvest. He thought to himself, 'What shall I do? I have no place to store my crops.'

"Then he said, 'This is what I'll do. I will tear down my barns and build bigger ones, and there I will store my surplus grain. And I'll say to myself, "You have plenty of grain laid up for many years. Take life easy; eat, drink and be merry."'

"But God said to him, 'You fool! This very night your life will be demanded from you. Then who will get what you have prepared for yourself?'

"This is how it will be with whoever stores up things for themselves but is not rich toward God."

LUKE 12:13–21

As people in affluent societies stock up on the latest smartphones and flat-screen TVs, it's hard to deny the increasing wealth in many parts of the world. You might call it "affluenza." There is anxiety, however, amid so much prosperity. It is the economic "puzzle of our time," said Robert J. Samuelson in *The Washington Post*. I wonder if this is true because we are attempting to find security in "more stuff"— stuff that is temporary and fleeting.

The Bible calls the pursuit of more stuff "greed." Jesus warned His followers about greed by telling a story about a rich man. The problem with this rich man was not that he had an abundance of bumper crops, or that he decided to build more storage space (Luke 12:16–18). The problem was that he invested his entire life in his possessions (v. 15). He drew his security from his material goods and failed to be "rich toward God" (v. 21). Rejecting the knowledge and precepts of God as the basis for life made him a fool. He was living for the moment while presuming on the future (vv. 19–20).

The "good life" cannot be found in things. Instead of seeking our security by acquiring "more stuff," may we find true satisfaction by investing our resources and our lives in and for God's kingdom.

―――

POVERTY OF PURPOSE IS WORSE
THAN POVERTY OF PURSE.

I will sing of your love and justice;
*   to you, L*ORD*, I will sing praise.*
I will be careful to lead a blameless life—
*   when will you come to me?*

I will conduct the affairs of my house
*   with a blameless heart.*
I will not look with approval
*   on anything that is vile.*

I hate what faithless people do;
*   I will have no part in it.*
The perverse of heart shall be far from me;
*   I will have nothing to do with what is evil.*

Whoever slanders their neighbor in secret,
*   I will put to silence;*
whoever has haughty eyes and a proud heart,
*   I will not tolerate.*

My eyes will be on the faithful in the land,
*   that they may dwell with me;*
the one whose walk is blameless
*   will minister to me.*

No one who practices deceit
*   will dwell in my house;*
no one who speaks falsely
*   will stand in my presence.*

Every morning I will put to silence
*   all the wicked in the land;*
I will cut off every evildoer
*   from the city of the L*ORD*.*

PSALM 101

A few years ago, officials in Philadelphia were astonished to receive a letter and payment from a motorist who had been given a speeding ticket in 1954. John Gedge, an English tourist, had been visiting the City of Brotherly Love when he was cited for speeding. The penalty was $15, but Gedge forgot about the ticket for almost 52 years until he discovered it in an old coat. "I thought, *I've got to pay it*," said Gedge, then 84 and the resident of a nursing home in East Sussex. "Englishmen pay their debts. My conscience is clear."

This story reminded me of the psalmist David's commitment to integrity. Although he made some terrible choices in his life, he declares his resolve to live blamelessly (Psalm 101). His integrity would begin in the privacy of his own house (v. 2) and extend to his choice of colleagues and friends (vv. 6–7). In sharp contrast to the corrupt lives of most kings of the ancient Near East, David had an integrity that led him to respect the life of his sworn enemy, King Saul (1 Samuel 24:4–6; 26:8–9).

As followers of Jesus, we are called to walk in integrity and to maintain a clear conscience. When we honor our commitments to God and to others, we will walk in fellowship with God. Our integrity will guide us (Proverbs 11:3) and help us walk securely (10:9).

———

THERE IS NO BETTER TEST OF
A MAN'S INTEGRITY THAN HIS BEHAVIOR
WHEN HE IS WRONG.

What then? Shall we sin because we are not under the law but under grace? By no means! Don't you know that when you offer yourselves to someone as obedient slaves, you are slaves of the one you obey—whether you are slaves to sin, which leads to death, or to obedience, which leads to righteousness? But thanks be to God that, though you used to be slaves to sin, you have come to obey from your heart the pattern of teaching that has now claimed your allegiance. You have been set free from sin and have become slaves to righteousness.

I am using an example from everyday life because of your human limitations. Just as you used to offer yourselves as slaves to impurity and to ever-increasing wickedness, so now offer yourselves as slaves to righteousness leading to holiness. When you were slaves to sin, you were free from the control of righteousness. What benefit did you reap at that time from the things you are now ashamed of? Those things result in death! But now that you have been set free from sin and have become slaves of God, the benefit you reap leads to holiness, and the result is eternal life. For the wages of sin is death, but the gift of God is eternal life in Christ Jesus our Lord.

ROMANS 6:15–23

On June 19, 1865, more than two years after President Abraham Lincoln had signed the Emancipation Proclamation, General Gordon Granger rode into Galveston, Texas, and read General Order Number 3: "The people of Texas are informed that, in accordance with a Proclamation from the Executive of the United States, all slaves are free." For the first time, slaves in Texas learned that they were already free. Some were shocked; many others celebrated. June 19 soon became known as "Juneteenth."

Nearly 25 years after the "Emancipation Proclamation" of the cross of Jesus, Paul wrote to the Roman believers. Some of them still did not understand what it meant to be free from sin's bondage. They thought they could go on sinning since they were under grace (Romans 6:15). So Paul reminded them of their status in Jesus by appealing to a familiar fact: Whatever we submit to becomes our master (John 8:34). To commit sin puts us in bondage to sin.

The other option is to be a slave of righteousness. Salvation actually means a change of bondage. As we once served sin, we are now committed to lives of righteousness because of the freedom Jesus provides.

My brothers and sisters, let us become in practice what we already are in status—free!

———

TRUE FREEDOM IS FOUND
IN BONDAGE TO CHRIST.

This is what happened during the time of Xerxes, the Xerxes who ruled over 127 provinces stretching from India to Cush: At that time King Xerxes reigned from his royal throne in the citadel of Susa, and in the third year of his reign he gave a banquet for all his nobles and officials. The military leaders of Persia and Media, the princes, and the nobles of the provinces were present.

For a full 180 days he displayed the vast wealth of his kingdom and the splendor and glory of his majesty. When these days were over, the king gave a banquet, lasting seven days, in the enclosed garden of the king's palace, for all the people from the least to the greatest who were in the citadel of Susa.

Queen Vashti also gave a banquet for the women in the royal palace of King Xerxes.

On the seventh day, when King Xerxes was in high spirits from wine, he commanded the seven eunuchs who served him—Mehuman, Biztha, Harbona, Bigtha, Abagtha, Zethar and Karkas—to bring before him Queen Vashti, wearing her royal crown, in order to display her beauty to the people and nobles, for she was lovely to look at. But when the attendants delivered the king's command, Queen Vashti refused to come. Then the king became furious and burned with anger.

ESTHER 1:1–5, 9–12

In 1967, American vocalist Aretha Franklin topped the charts with her hit single "Respect." The song became an inspirational anthem for the civil rights movement and for others who demanded to be treated with respect.

Long before Aretha's hit record, Queen Vashti topped the Persian charts with her own version of "Respect." The book of Esther begins with King Ahasuerus hosting a great celebration. In addition to displaying his wealth and power, he also wanted to showcase his wife's beauty. So he commanded that Queen Vashti be brought before him and his guests.

If she obeyed, she would have allowed the king to degrade and disrespect her. If she refused, she risked losing her life. She refused. What courage! Vashti didn't want to compromise her character by being reduced to a piece of property. Her desire for respect led to her banishment. We have no record that Vashti feared the Lord. But her courage shows that she understood the God-given dignity accorded to every human being.

God created us in His image and crowned us with glory and honor, having made us "a little lower than the angels" (Psalm 8:5). Out of love and reverence for Him, let us treat others—and ourselves—with honor, dignity, and respect.

GOD DESIRES THAT WE SHOW
RESPECT TO ALL PEOPLE,
BECAUSE EVERYONE BEARS HIS IMAGE.

*If anyone is poor among your fellow Israelites in any of
the towns of the land the LORD your God is giving you, do
not be hardhearted or tightfisted toward them. Rather, be
openhanded and freely lend them whatever they need. Be
careful not to harbor this wicked thought: "The seventh year,
the year for canceling debts, is near," so that you do not show
ill will toward the needy among your fellow Israelites and give
them nothing. They may then appeal to the LORD against
you, and you will be found guilty of sin. Give generously
to them and do so without a grudging heart; then because
of this the LORD your God will bless you in all your work
and in everything you put your hand to. There will always
be poor people in the land. Therefore I command you to be
openhanded toward your fellow Israelites who are poor and
needy in your land.*

DEUTERONOMY 15:7–11

Francis Chan, in his book *Crazy Love*, tells of a family with an interesting Christmas tradition. On Christmas morning, the Robynson family doesn't focus on opening presents under the Christmas tree. Instead, they make pancakes and coffee, and they serve the breakfast to the homeless. This is a small but creative way to show God's love and generosity to the poor.

God expected this kind of generosity from His people. In Deuteronomy 15, Moses emphasized the reality of poverty and how the more affluent must deal with it. They were warned of four dangers:

+ A hard heart, ignoring the needs of the poor (v. 7).

+ A closed hand, withholding what the poor lacked (v. 7).

+ An evil thought, hesitating or refusing to loan money to the poor because the year of canceling debts was nearing (v. 9).

+ A grudging spirit, a reluctance to satisfy the needs of the poor among them (v. 10). Not only were they warned about selfishness but more important they were also encouraged to be spontaneously generous (vv. 8, 10, 11).

Among God's people, there must always be a spirit of generosity toward the poor. Let's open our hearts and our hands to those in need.

———

GENEROSITY STEMS FROM THE HEART
THAT HAS EXPERIENCED GOD'S GRACE.

Then Ananias went to the house and entered it. Placing his hands on Saul, he said, "Brother Saul, the Lord—Jesus, who appeared to you on the road as you were coming here—has sent me so that you may see again and be filled with the Holy Spirit." Immediately, something like scales fell from Saul's eyes, and he could see again. He got up and was baptized, and after taking some food, he regained his strength.

Saul spent several days with the disciples in Damascus. At once he began to preach in the synagogues that Jesus is the Son of God. All those who heard him were astonished and asked, "Isn't he the man who raised havoc in Jerusalem among those who call on this name? And hasn't he come here to take them as prisoners to the chief priests?" Yet Saul grew more and more powerful and baffled the Jews living in Damascus by proving that Jesus is the Messiah.

After many days had gone by, there was a conspiracy among the Jews to kill him, but Saul learned of their plan. Day and night they kept close watch on the city gates in order to kill him. But his followers took him by night and lowered him in a basket through an opening in the wall.

When he came to Jerusalem, he tried to join the disciples, but they were all afraid of him, not believing that he really was a disciple. But Barnabas took him and brought him to the apostles. He told them how Saul on his journey had seen the Lord and that the Lord had spoken to him, and how in Damascus he had preached fearlessly in the name of Jesus.

ACTS 9:17–27

A new believer recently attended a worship service at the church where I am pastor. He had long, multicolored, spiked hair. He was dressed in dark clothes and had many piercings and tattoos. Some stared, and others just gave him that "It's good to see you in church, but please don't sit next to me" smile. Yet there were some during the greeting time who went out of their way to welcome and accept him. I call them "bridge builders."

Barnabas was that bridge builder for Saul (also called Paul). When Saul arrived in Jerusalem three years after his conversion, many disciples were afraid of him and doubted his transformation (Acts 9:26). And it was for good reason that He didn't receive a warm welcome from the Jerusalem church greeters. Saul had a terrible reputation for persecuting Christians! But Barnabas, a Jewish convert, believed God's work of grace in Saul's life and became a bridge between him and the apostles (v. 27).

Saul needed someone to come alongside him to encourage him, teach him, and introduce him to other believers. Barnabas was that bridge. As a result, Saul was brought into deeper fellowship with the disciples in Jerusalem and was able to preach the gospel there freely and boldly.

New believers need a Barnabas in their lives. Find ways to be a bridge in the lives of others.

———

BE A BRIDGE OF ENCOURAGEMENT
TO SOMEONE TODAY.

Two are better than one,
*   because they have a good return for their labor:*
If either of them falls down,
*   one can help the other up.*
But pity anyone who falls
*   and has no one to help them up.*
Also, if two lie down together, they will keep warm.
*   But how can one keep warm alone?*
Though one may be overpowered,
*   two can defend themselves.*
A cord of three strands is not quickly broken.

ECCLESIASTES 4:9–12

While promoting the film *Rocky Balboa*, Sylvester Stallone surprised Christians with what he revealed. He said that his faith in Jesus Christ had influenced the writing of the first Rocky film and that his decision to create the final movie was inspired by his renewed affiliation with Christianity. As part of this transformation, Stallone realized that a poor choice had previously guided his life—self-reliance. He says, "You need to have the expertise and the guidance of someone else." Stallone learned something that many people are beginning to acknowledge—we need God and we need other people.

The Bible confirms our need for God and others. David expressed his reliance on God through crying out to Him and pleading with Him in prayer. "Hear my cry for help, my King and my God, for to you I pray" (Psalm 5:2). And in Ecclesiastes we read that Solomon encouraged a proper reliance on others. In fact, he said helping each other can strengthen us, but individualism and self-reliance are dangerous and make for weakness. Two acting together are better than one self-reliant individual (4:9–12).

God gave us each other. Let's passionately rely on His power and draw from the help of others.

———

WE CAN GO A LOT FURTHER TOGETHER
THAN WE CAN GO ALONE.

Then Moses led Israel from the Red Sea and they went into the Desert of Shur. For three days they traveled in the desert without finding water. When they came to Marah, they could not drink its water because it was bitter. (That is why the place is called Marah.) So the people grumbled against Moses, saying, "What are we to drink?"

Then Moses cried out to the LORD, and the LORD showed him a piece of wood. He threw it into the water, and the water became fit to drink.

There the LORD issued a ruling and instruction for them and put them to the test. He said, "If you listen carefully to the LORD your God and do what is right in his eyes, if you pay attention to his commands and keep all his decrees, I will not bring on you any of the diseases I brought on the Egyptians, for I am the LORD, who heals you."

Then they came to Elim, where there were twelve springs and seventy palm trees, and they camped there near the water.

EXODUS 15:22–27

The children of Israel had not gone far from the shore of the Red Sea when the realities of their new freedom began to register. They no longer enjoyed the ample food and water supply of Egypt. Now, after traveling three days into the wilderness, the large crowd had no water. And when they finally arrived at the oasis of Marah, the water was bitter (Exodus 15:23).

Thus the children of Israel were compelled to rely on a miracle. So they cried out to Moses, and Moses cried out to the Lord. The Lord showed him a piece of wood, which Moses cast into the water. Miraculously, the water turned sweet.

The transformation of the water was a miracle akin to the plague of blood sent to Pharaoh and the Egyptians (Exodus 7:14–25). Egypt's clean water had been sullied with blood by the hand of the Lord. The lesson of Marah was clear—the same hand that turned water into blood could turn bitter water into sweet. The same power that brought curses on Egypt could bring health to Israel.

If you have a seemingly impossible need today, remember that the hand that supplied your greatest need—forgiveness of sin—is the same hand that can adequately supply all your needs. Trust God to accomplish things that seem impossible.

IMPOSSIBILITIES COMPEL US
TO RELY ON GOD.

"Be careful not to practice your righteousness in front of others to be seen by them. If you do, you will have no reward from your Father in heaven.

"So when you give to the needy, do not announce it with trumpets, as the hypocrites do in the synagogues and on the streets, to be honored by others. Truly I tell you, they have received their reward in full. But when you give to the needy, do not let your left hand know what your right hand is doing, so that your giving may be in secret. Then your Father, who sees what is done in secret, will reward you."

MATTHEW 6:1–4

"What ever happened to the notion of giving for the sake of giving?" asked Tim Harford, columnist for *Financial Times*. "The closer you look at charitable giving, the less charitable it appears to be." A study of door-to-door fund-raising campaigns, for instance, found that organizations earned far more by selling lottery tickets than by asking for donations.

"This hardly suggests a world populated by altruists seeking to do the maximum good with their charitable cash," said Harford. At least for some people, there's a something-for-me/something-for-you approach to giving.

Jesus also dealt with the issue of motives in giving. When He said not to let your left hand know what your right hand is doing, He was teaching that our motives for giving to God and to others must be pure. Our giving should be in response to God's love. To encourage pure motives, Jesus instructed people to give and to do other good deeds in secret—with no thought of themselves. God, who sees everything, would reward them (Matthew 6:3–4).

Our generosity should be God-centered—not to make us look good but to please the Lord. With your next good deed, ask yourself: If I knew no one would ever find out I did this, would I still do it?

———

GOD SEES THE GIVER AS WELL AS THE GIFT—
THE HEART AS WELL AS THE HAND.

Come, let us sing for joy to the LORD;
  let us shout aloud to the Rock of our salvation.
Let us come before him with thanksgiving
  and extol him with music and song.

For the LORD is the great God,
  the great King above all gods.
In his hand are the depths of the earth,
  and the mountain peaks belong to him.
The sea is his, for he made it,
  and his hands formed the dry land.

Come, let us bow down in worship,
  let us kneel before the LORD our Maker;
for he is our God and we are the people of his pasture,
  the flock under his care.

Today, if only you would hear his voice,
"Do not harden your hearts as you did at Meribah,
  as you did that day at Massah in the wilderness,
where your ancestors tested me;
  they tried me, though they had seen what I did.
For forty years I was angry with that generation;
  I said, 'They are a people whose hearts go astray,
  and they have not known my ways.'
So I declared on oath in my anger,
  'They shall never enter my rest.'"

PSALM 95

36

The ancient Greeks and Romans rejected kneeling as a part of their worship. They said that kneeling was unworthy of a free man—unsuitable for the culture of Greece and appropriate only for barbarians. The scholars Plutarch and Theophrastus regarded kneeling as an expression of superstition. Aristotle called it a barbaric form of behavior. This belief, however, was never held by God's people.

In Psalm 95:6, the psalmist indicated that kneeling expressed a deep reverence for God. In this one verse he used three different Hebrew words to express what the attitude and position of the worshiper should be.

First, he used the word *bow*. This means to sink down to one's knees, giving respect to the Lord. The second word he used was *worship*, which means to fall prostrate as a sign of honor to the Lord, with an associated meaning of allegiance to Him. The psalmist then used the word *kneel*, which means to be on one's knees giving praise to God.

According to the psalmist, kneeling in God's presence is a sign of reverence rather than a barbaric form of behavior. The important thing, however, is not just our physical position but also a humble posture of the heart.

———

OUR ATTITUDE IN WORSHIP
MATTERS FAR MORE THAN
THE POSITION OF OUR WORSHIP.

Keep on loving one another as brothers and sisters. Do not forget to show hospitality to strangers, for by so doing some people have shown hospitality to angels without knowing it. Continue to remember those in prison as if you were together with them in prison, and those who are mistreated as if you yourselves were suffering.

Marriage should be honored by all, and the marriage bed kept pure, for God will judge the adulterer and all the sexually immoral. Keep your lives free from the love of money and be content with what you have, because God has said, "Never will I leave you; never will I forsake you."

So we say with confidence, "The Lord is my helper; I will not be afraid. What can mere mortals do to me?"

HEBREWS 13:1–6

A few years ago, Casey Fenton co-founded a nonprofit service that helps travelers find a "friendlier alternative" to unfriendly hotels. They find homeowners who are willing to offer their spare beds and couches to others.

The group boasts of almost a quarter of a million friendships that have been formed from their service. "The more we network," said Fenton, "the better chance we have of this world being a better place."

That service sounds a lot like biblical hospitality. In the final pages of his letter to the Hebrews, the writer instructed believers to practice their faith in Jesus Christ through hospitality (13:2). That was defined by the early Christ-followers as acts of generosity toward strangers.

In the first century, hospitality often included housing a guest. This was hardest to do during a time of persecution. These believers would not know whether the person was a spy or a fellow believer being pursued. But by entertaining strangers, the writer said, they could indeed be inviting a blessing into their homes.

As God's people, we are called to be hospitable to others as part of our gratitude for the salvation we have received from God.

PEOPLE WITH A HEART FOR GOD
HAVE A HEART FOR PEOPLE.

I am the LORD your God, who brought you out of Egypt, out of the land of slavery. You shall have no other gods before me.

You shall not make for yourself an image in the form of anything in heaven above or on the earth beneath or in the waters below. You shall not bow down to them or worship them; for I, the LORD your God, am a jealous God....

You shall not misuse the name of the LORD your God, for the LORD will not hold anyone guiltless who misuses his name.

Remember the Sabbath day by keeping it holy. Six days you shall labor and do all your work, but the seventh day is a sabbath to the LORD your God. On it you shall not do any work, neither you, nor your son or daughter, nor your male or female servant, nor your animals, nor any foreigner residing in your towns. For in six days the LORD made the heavens and the earth, the sea, and all that is in them, but he rested on the seventh day. Therefore the LORD blessed the Sabbath day and made it holy.

Honor your father and your mother, so that you may live long in the land the LORD your God is giving you.

You shall not murder.

You shall not commit adultery.

You shall not steal.

You shall not give false testimony against your neighbor.

You shall not covet your neighbor's house. You shall not covet your neighbor's wife, or his male or female servant, his ox or donkey, or anything that belongs to your neighbor.

EXODUS 20:1–17

Professional integrity and a commitment to excellence are the working philosophies that guide us on a daily basis." This is one of the introductory sentences from a website designed to provide fictional explanations, fake employment references, and verification for unexcused absences. A more accurate sentence would be "professional lying and commitment to providing false testimony are what guide us daily."

The ninth commandment was designed to protect the Israelite community from such falsehood (Exodus 20:16). When Moses said, "You shall not give false testimony against your neighbor," he was telling them not to deceive a close community companion. The Israelites were to avoid coloring a situation with falsehood to protect themselves, such as lies that ruined reputations, half-truths, and boastful exaggerations.

The basic truth of this instruction is that we need personal integrity in our relationships. This command was so important because behind all truth we find the Lord's character, which cannot be false. Likewise, God wanted His covenant community to deal truthfully with one another. The consequences of not obeying this command were a diluted, weak community and, ultimately, God's judgment (Psalm 5:6).

How do we live out this commandment today? It begins with developing a deeper reverence for the character of God (Exodus 20:20). Our fear of God helps us to remain truthful and blameless.

NOTHING WEAKENS THE TRUTH
MORE THAN STRETCHING IT.

Then the Pharisees went out and laid plans to trap him in his words. They sent their disciples to him along with the Herodians. "Teacher," they said, "we know that you are a man of integrity and that you teach the way of God in accordance with the truth. You aren't swayed by others, because you pay no attention to who they are. Tell us then, what is your opinion? Is it right to pay the imperial tax to Caesar or not?"

But Jesus, knowing their evil intent, said, "You hypocrites, why are you trying to trap me? Show me the coin used for paying the tax." They brought him a denarius, and he asked them, "Whose image is this? And whose inscription?"

"Caesar's," they replied.

Then he said to them, "So give back to Caesar what is Caesar's, and to God what is God's."

When they heard this, they were amazed. So they left him and went away.

MATTHEW 22:15–22

In a report in *USA Today*, Rick Hampson wrote: "The young generally don't have the old-time political religion. They look at voting and see a quaint, irrational act." One graduate was quoted as saying, "I don't care enough to care about why I don't care." I wonder if this is how we as Jesus-followers sometimes view our civic responsibility!

The insights of Jesus in Matthew 22 helped His followers think clearly about their civic duty in the world. The Jews were required to pay taxes to the Roman government. They hated this taxation because the money went directly into Caesar's treasury, where some of it supported the pagan temples and decadent lifestyle of the Roman aristocracy. They may have questioned whether they even had a civic responsibility to Caesar. Jesus reminded them, however, that they had dual citizenship. They lived in a world with two kingdoms—Caesar's kingdom (human authority) and God's kingdom (spiritual authority). They had responsibilities to both, but their greater responsibility was to God and His kingdom (Acts 5:28–29).

As followers of Christ, we are commanded to cooperate with our rulers, but we are called to give God our ultimate obedience and commitment.

———

GOVERNMENT HAS AUTHORITY,
BUT GOD HAS ULTIMATE AUTHORITY.

My son, if you accept my words and store up my commands within you,
turning your ear to wisdom and applying your heart to understanding—
indeed, if you call out for insight and cry aloud for understanding,
and if you look for it as for silver and search for it as for hidden treasure,
then you will understand the fear of the LORD and find the knowledge
    of God.
For the LORD gives wisdom; from his mouth come knowledge and
    understanding.
He holds success in store for the upright, he is a shield to those whose
    walk is blameless,
for he guards the course of the just and protects the way of his faithful
    ones.
Then you will understand what is right and just and fair—every good
    path.
For wisdom will enter your heart, and knowledge will be pleasant to
    your soul.
Discretion will protect you, and understanding will guard you.
Wisdom will save you from the ways of wicked men, from men whose
    words are perverse,
who have left the straight paths to walk in dark ways,
who delight in doing wrong and rejoice in the perverseness of evil,
whose paths are crooked and who are devious in their ways.
Wisdom will save you also from the adulterous woman, from the
    wayward woman with her seductive words, who has left the partner
    of her youth and ignored the covenant she made before God.

PROVERBS 2:1–17

When Betty Goldstein of Staten Island, New York, entered the hospital, her husband Ron wrapped her 3.5-carat diamond ring in a napkin for safekeeping. But in a forgetful moment, Goldstein threw the napkin in the trash. When he realized his mistake, he dashed outside, only to see the garbage truck rumbling down the street. So he called the local sanitation department and got permission to follow the truck to a transfer station. Workers began sorting through hundreds of garbage bags and recovered the ring an hour later.

The writer of Proverbs urges us to search diligently for something far more precious—wisdom. In chapter 2, a father encourages his son to do whatever is necessary to get insight and wisdom. This strenuous search for wisdom is actually a search for God himself (vv. 3–5). In fact, inner happiness comes when man attains this wisdom (3:13). He encourages his son to search diligently for this rare jewel, because wisdom is not usually discovered by the casual observer. Wisdom is discovered and enjoyed only by those who are diligent, devoted, and determined to seek it.

Let us devote our whole being to searching for that rare jewel of wisdom.

———

GET WISDOM.
THOUGH IT COST ALL YOU HAVE,
GET UNDERSTANDING.
—Solomon

For this reason, since the day we heard about you, we have not stopped praying for you. We continually ask God to fill you with the knowledge of his will through all the wisdom and understanding that the Spirit gives, so that you may live a life worthy of the Lord and please him in every way: bearing fruit in every good work, growing in the knowledge of God, being strengthened with all power according to his glorious might so that you may have great endurance and patience, and giving joyful thanks to the Father, who has qualified you to share in the inheritance of his holy people in the kingdom of light. For he has rescued us from the dominion of darkness and brought us into the kingdom of the Son he loves, in whom we have redemption, the forgiveness of sins.

COLOSSIANS 1:9–14

If you keep in touch with family and friends through the postal service, you probably have received or sent a change of address notice. It goes something like this: "I will no longer be receiving mail at _____. My new address will be _____. Thank you for making a note of this change."

Paul reminded the believers in Colosse that they had "a change of address" and that they should share it with others. They had been moved from one community and "conveyed" or transplanted, by the grace of God, into a new community. They had been rescued from the kingdom of darkness and had been brought into the kingdom of Jesus (1:13). In e-mail terms, their old address was sinner@kingdomofdarkness. But when they became followers of Jesus, their new address became saved@kingdomofHisdearSon.

In Philippians 3:20, Paul declared that all believers are citizens of heaven and should live worthy of their new address. He encouraged the Christians in Colosse to walk in wisdom toward those who were outside the faith. In that way people could see and hear about the changes (Colossians 4:5–6).

If you have had "a change of address," tell someone about what Jesus has done in you.

———

WHEN JESUS COMES INTO A LIFE,
HE CHANGES EVERYTHING.

Do not take advantage of the widow or the fatherless. If you do and they cry out to me, I will certainly hear their cry. My anger will be aroused, and I will kill you with the sword; your wives will become widows and your children fatherless.

EXODUS 22:22–24

A CNN report estimated that there are approximately 40 million widows in India. Fifteen thousand of them live on the streets of the northern city of Vrindavan. Unfortunately, many of their families do not hear their cries. A 70-year-old widow says, "My son tells me: 'You have grown old. Now who is going to feed you? Go away.'" She cries, "What do I do? My pain has no limit."

During the time of the Exodus, when God gave His people instructions in the desert, He told them they had a responsibility to care for widows and fatherless children in the land (Exodus 22:22–24). They were to leave some of the harvest in the field for them, and every third year they took up a special tithe for the needy. God expected His people to hear the cries of the powerless, defend their rights, and care for them.

The Israelites were commanded to care for others as a remembrance of their experience in Egypt. When they were in trouble and cried out to God, He heard their cries and helped them. So their memory of oppression and release was intended to mold their values, attitudes, and actions toward the powerless in the land (Deuteronomy 24:18–22).

Let us imitate our Father by hearing the cries of the needy in our world.

———

THE CLOSER YOU ARE TO GOD,
THE MORE YOU'LL HAVE A HEART FOR OTHERS.

For we know that if the earthly tent we live in is destroyed, we have a building from God, an eternal house in heaven, not built by human hands. Meanwhile we groan, longing to be clothed instead with our heavenly dwelling, because when we are clothed, we will not be found naked. For while we are in this tent, we groan and are burdened, because we do not wish to be unclothed but to be clothed instead with our heavenly dwelling, so that what is mortal may be swallowed up by life. Now the one who has fashioned us for this very purpose is God, who has given us the Spirit as a deposit, guaranteeing what is to come.

Therefore we are always confident and know that as long as we are at home in the body we are away from the Lord. For we live by faith, not by sight. We are confident, I say, and would prefer to be away from the body and at home with the Lord.

2 CORINTHIANS 5:1–8

At least a dozen multimillionaires have left money to themselves in hope of being brought back to life. These immortality seekers have arranged to be cryogenically frozen after death, reports *The Wall Street Journal*. They've also put their wealth in "personal revival trusts," which they believe will be waiting for them when scientists resuscitate them in the future.

Even if resuscitation were possible, to seek eternal life apart from the One who is immortal is to chase an elusive dream.

Paul affirmed that the Lord alone is the source of immortality (1 Timothy 6:16). He is everlasting in His character and actions. For human beings, however, death is universal, inevitable, and ultimately leads to judgment (Hebrews 9:27). This is all a result of our sin, and it can be countered only by the redemption through Jesus Christ (John 3:15–16). Through His resurrection, Jesus broke the power of death and showed humanity the way to immortality (2 Timothy 1:10).

Our response to our mortality should not be to preserve our physical bodies through cryogenics, but to be ready for our own death by receiving the gift of eternal life in Jesus.

———

TO LIVE FOREVER,
WE MUST INVITE JESUS
TO LIVE IN US NOW.

Even so the body is not made up of one part but of many. Now if the foot should say, "Because I am not a hand, I do not belong to the body," it would not for that reason stop being part of the body. And if the ear should say, "Because I am not an eye, I do not belong to the body," it would not for that reason stop being part of the body. If the whole body were an eye, where would the sense of hearing be? If the whole body were an ear, where would the sense of smell be? But in fact God has placed the parts in the body, every one of them, just as he wanted them to be. If they were all one part, where would the body be? As it is, there are many parts, but one body.

The eye cannot say to the hand, "I don't need you!" And the head cannot say to the feet, "I don't need you!" On the contrary, those parts of the body that seem to be weaker are indispensable, and the parts that we think are less honorable we treat with special honor. And the parts that are unpresentable are treated with special modesty, while our presentable parts need no special treatment. But God has put the body together, giving greater honor to the parts that lacked it, so that there should be no division in the body, but that its parts should have equal concern for each other. If one part suffers, every part suffers with it; if one part is honored, every part rejoices with it.

1 CORINTHIANS 12:14–26

The story has been told about a conductor who was rehearsing his orchestra. The organ was giving a beautiful melody, the drums were thundering, the trumpets were blaring, and the violins were singing beautifully. But the conductor noticed something missing—the piccolo. The piccolo player had gotten distracted and hoped his instrument wouldn't be missed. The conductor reminded him: "Each one of us is necessary."

This was essentially the same message Paul communicated to the Corinthian believers in his first letter to them (12:4–7). Every Christian plays an important role in the body of Christ. Paul gave a list of gifts of the Spirit and compared their use to the functioning of the various parts of the human body for the good of the whole (vv. 8–10). The Corinthian believers may have had different cultural backgrounds, gifts, and personalities, but they were filled with the same Spirit and belonged to the same body of Christ. Paul made special mention of the parts of the body that were weak and obscure, and he taught that all believers have a necessary and significant role. No one part was more necessary than any other.

Remember, Jesus has given you a significant part to play and will use you to build up His people.

———

AS A MEMBER OF THE BODY OF CHRIST,
YOU ARE A NECESSARY PART OF THE WHOLE.

Thus the heavens and the earth were completed in all their vast array.

By the seventh day God had finished the work he had been doing; so on the seventh day he rested from all his work. Then God blessed the seventh day and made it holy, because on it he rested from all the work of creating that he had done.

GENESIS 2:1–3

We live in an action-oriented world, and it seems that simplifying our lives has never been more complicated! Doesn't it seem that there's always work to do and no time for rest? Answer the following questions as honestly as you can to determine if you need to rest: Do I feel stressed when functioning in my normal day-to-day activities? Is it difficult to find joy? Do I get the kind of rest my body needs? Do I wake up tired?

In creation, God established a pattern of work and rest, which is a model for believers. For six days God worked to bring order to our world. But on the seventh day, after He had finished all His creative activity, He rested. God showed us that rest is appropriate and right.

Jesus demonstrated the importance of rest when He sat wearily beside a well after a long walk (John 4:6) and when He slept in the back of a boat with His head on a pillow (Mark 4:38). He also rested when He and His disciples got away from the crowds (Mark 6:31–32).

If the Lord rested from the work of creation and from His earthly ministry, we need to rest from our work as well. Our times of rest refresh us for times of service. Schedule some "slow down" time this week.

———

ALL WORK AND NO PLAY
WILL TAKE THE JOY OF LIFE AWAY.

"Do not judge, or you too will be judged. For in the same way you judge others, you will be judged, and with the measure you use, it will be measured to you.

"Why do you look at the speck of sawdust in your brother's eye and pay no attention to the plank in your own eye? How can you say to your brother, 'Let me take the speck out of your eye,' when all the time there is a plank in your own eye? You hypocrite, first take the plank out of your own eye, and then you will see clearly to remove the speck from your brother's eye."

MATTHEW 7:1–5

I normally take my kids to school thirty minutes before class begins. One morning we left the house later than normal. When we picked them up from school, my middle son insisted that they had not made it to class on time, and he had proof. He proudly presented Exhibit A: He had seen his sister with a detention slip in her hand. The only problem with his evidence was that it was not *her* detention for being late to school—it was her classmate's. She was holding it for him until he finished tying his shoe. My son apologized for misjudging his sister. He learned an important lesson about not judging others.

When Jesus began teaching His followers, He made sure they learned the same lesson (Matthew 7:1). When He gave the "don't judge" command, however, He wasn't saying to refuse to examine people's actions in order to hold them accountable to God's standards. He simply wanted them to refrain from judging others just to build themselves up. Those who judged others would find themselves being judged in the same manner by God and by others.

There are several reasons Jesus told His followers not to judge others. First, they may have only known part of the story (1 Corinthians 4:5). Second, when they judged others, they brought God's judgment on themselves (Romans 2:1–3). Third, God is the only One who is qualified to judge anyone (James 4:11–12).

Before we judge others, let's seek to understand the issues and motives of the situation. Then, let's examine our own lives and humbly love, forgive, and help others in a spirit of grace.

———

YOU DON'T GET CLOSER TO GOD
BY PASSING JUDGMENT ON OTHERS.

"Therefore I tell you, do not worry about your life, what you will eat or drink; or about your body, what you will wear. Is not life more than food, and the body more than clothes? Look at the birds of the air; they do not sow or reap or store away in barns, and yet your heavenly Father feeds them. Are you not much more valuable than they? Can any one of you by worrying add a single hour to your life?

"And why do you worry about clothes? See how the flowers of the field grow. They do not labor or spin. Yet I tell you that not even Solomon in all his splendor was dressed like one of these. If that is how God clothes the grass of the field, which is here today and tomorrow is thrown into the fire, will he not much more clothe you—you of little faith? So do not worry, saying, 'What shall we eat?' or 'What shall we drink?' or 'What shall we wear?' For the pagans run after all these things, and your heavenly Father knows that you need them. But seek first his kingdom and his righteousness, and all these things will be given to you as well."

MATTHEW 6:25–33

In a recent year, my family had much to worry about. For one thing, my wife wasn't called back to her full-time teaching position (we counted on her income), my son was having recurring chest pain, our insurance was running out and an alternative plan was too expensive, and—if that wasn't enough—I changed jobs. At some point these concerns turned into worry, and we let them consume us. We desperately needed the wisdom Jesus spoke of in Matthew 6.

That section gave His followers four reasons why they shouldn't worry:

1. *Life is more than food, drink, and clothing* (v. 25). Jesus understood that these are necessities in life, but they aren't the most important things in life.
2. *God cares for His children* (v. 26). He feeds the birds and clothes the flowers—how much more does God care for those created in His image?
3. *Worrying doesn't accomplish anything* (v. 27). Jesus said that worrying doesn't add anything useful to the worrier's day; it's actually a life-draining endeavor.
4. *Worrying is godless* (v. 32). Jesus wants His disciples to live with the assurance that their heavenly Father is in complete control.

Focus on what God cares about, and He will take care of what you worry about (v. 33). And pursue His rule and supremacy in your life. When you do that, He will take care of your needs.

WHEN WE PUT OUR CARES INTO HIS HANDS,
HE PUTS HIS PEACE INTO OUR HEARTS.

Now faith is confidence in what we hope for and assurance about what we do not see. This is what the ancients were commended for.

By faith we understand that the universe was formed at God's command, so that what is seen was not made out of what was visible.

By faith Abel brought God a better offering than Cain did. By faith he was commended as righteous, when God spoke well of his offerings. And by faith Abel still speaks, even though he is dead.

By faith Enoch was taken from this life, so that he did not experience death: "He could not be found, because God had taken him away." For before he was taken, he was commended as one who pleased God. And without faith it is impossible to please God, because anyone who comes to him must believe that he exists and that he rewards those who earnestly seek him.

HEBREWS 11:1–6

A *National Geographic News* survey reported that many young Americans are geographically illiterate. According to the survey, 63 percent of Americans aged 18–24 failed to correctly locate Iraq on a map of the Middle East. The results for US geography are even more dismal. Half could not find New York State on the map, a third could not find Louisiana, and 48 percent could not locate Mississippi.

Understanding geography is helpful in daily life, but "God-ography" (finding God) is infinitely more crucial—for now and for eternity.

In Hebrews 11:6 we are told that to find God and please Him, we first have to believe that He exists. How can we prove that God exists? Finding God is a matter of faith—confidence in Him and commitment to Him. This confidence and commitment should remain strong even though the objects of our faith are unseen. The writer of Hebrews and the apostle John agree that ultimately the way to find the Lord and please Him is by believing in His Son Jesus (Hebrews 11:6; John 14:6).

Finding God is solely a work of God. Those who seek Him will find Him because God will give them a heart to recognize Him as Lord (Jeremiah 29:13–14).

———

TO FIND GOD,
WE MUST BE WILLING TO SEEK HIM.

Wives, submit yourselves to your own husbands as you do to the Lord. For the husband is the head of the wife as Christ is the head of the church, his body, of which he is the Savior. Now as the church submits to Christ, so also wives should submit to their husbands in everything.

Husbands, love your wives, just as Christ loved the church and gave himself up for her to make her holy, cleansing her by the washing with water through the word, and to present her to himself as a radiant church, without stain or wrinkle or any other blemish, but holy and blameless. In this same way, husbands ought to love their wives as their own bodies. He who loves his wife loves himself. After all, no one ever hated their own body, but they feed and care for their body, just as Christ does the church—for we are members of his body. "For this reason a man will leave his father and mother and be united to his wife, and the two will become one flesh." This is a profound mystery—but I am talking about Christ and the church. However, each one of you also must love his wife as he loves himself, and the wife must respect her husband.

EPHESIANS 5:22–33

When my wife had dental surgery, she was out of commission for the weekend. While she was recuperating, I had the daunting task of taking care of her and the kids. I cooked, washed dishes, made special trips to the store for her, and bathed the kids. When I saw all I had done, I thought to myself, *I deserve extra credit and reciprocal service when she gets better*. Before I gave myself too many pats on the back, however, the Holy Spirit reminded me that what I was doing was my privilege and duty as a Christian husband.

In Paul's time, many believed that the husband's needs dominated the household and that the wife existed to fulfill his needs and to serve him. The Christian view was quite different, however. Women were seen as persons of equal worth. The wife was transformed from being an accessory to being a person of intrinsic value—and the focus of her husband's concern. Instead of demanding that she live for him, he was to serve her!

Ephesians 5:25 portrays Christ as loving the church and giving himself for her. And verse 29 indicates that Jesus nourishes and cares for her. As husbands pursue Christlikeness, they have the privilege and duty to nurture, take care of, and sacrifice for their wives.

———

IF YOU THINK IT'S POSSIBLE
TO LOVE YOUR WIFE TOO MUCH,
YOU PROBABLY HAVEN'T LOVED HER ENOUGH.

Jesus knew that the Father had put all things under his power, and that he had come from God and was returning to God; so he got up from the meal, took off his outer clothing, and wrapped a towel around his waist. After that, he poured water into a basin and began to wash his disciples' feet, drying them with the towel that was wrapped around him.

He came to Simon Peter, who said to him, "Lord, are you going to wash my feet?"

Jesus replied, "You do not realize now what I am doing, but later you will understand."

"No," said Peter, "you shall never wash my feet."

Jesus answered, "Unless I wash you, you have no part with me."

"Then, Lord," Simon Peter replied, "not just my feet but my hands and my head as well!"

Jesus answered, "Those who have had a bath need only to wash their feet; their whole body is clean. And you are clean, though not every one of you." For he knew who was going to betray him, and that was why he said not every one was clean.

When he had finished washing their feet, he put on his clothes and returned to his place. "Do you understand what I have done for you?" he asked them. "You call me 'Teacher' and 'Lord,' and rightly so, for that is what I am. Now that I, your Lord and Teacher, have washed your feet, you also should wash one another's feet. I have set you an example that you should do as I have done for you."

JOHN 13:3–15

Pay It Forward is a movie about a twelve-year-old's plan to make a difference in the world. Motivated by a teacher at his school, Trevor invites a homeless man to sleep in his garage. Unaware of this arrangement, his mother awakens one evening to find the man working on her truck. Holding him at gunpoint, she asks him to explain himself. He shows her that he has successfully repaired her truck and tells her about Trevor's kindness. He says, "I'm just paying it forward."

I think this is the concept Jesus had in mind in one of His last conversations with His disciples. He wanted to show them the full extent of His love. So before their last meal together, He took off His outer garment, wrapped a towel around His waist, and began to wash His disciples' feet. This was shocking because only slaves washed feet. It was an act of servanthood and a symbol that pointed to Jesus's sacrifice, passion, and humiliation on the cross. His request to His disciples was this: "Now that I, your Lord and Teacher, have washed your feet, you also should wash one another's feet" (John 13:14). They were to "pay it forward."

Imagine how different our world would look if we gave the kind of love to others that God has given us through Jesus.

———

TO KNOW LOVE, OPEN YOUR HEART TO JESUS.
TO SHOW LOVE, OPEN YOUR HEART TO OTHERS.

When [Josiah] heard the words of the Book of the Law, he tore his robes. He gave these orders ... "Go and inquire of the LORD for me and for the people and for all Judah about what is written in this book that has been found. Great is the LORD's anger that burns against us because those who have gone before us have not obeyed the words of this book; they have not acted in accordance with all that is written there concerning us."

... The prophet Huldah, who ... lived in Jerusalem, in the New Quarter ... said to them, "This is what the LORD, the God of Israel, says: Tell the man who sent you to me, 'This is what the LORD says: I am going to bring disaster on this place and its people, according to everything written in the book the king of Judah has read. Because they have forsaken me and burned incense to other gods ... my anger will burn against this place. Because you tore your robes and wept in my presence, I also have heard you, declares the LORD. Therefore I will gather you to your ancestors, and you will be buried in peace....'"

So they took her answer back to the king.

Then the king called together all ... the people of Judah, the inhabitants of Jerusalem, the priests and the prophets.... He read in their hearing all the words of the Book of the Covenant, which had been found in the temple of the LORD. The king stood by the pillar and renewed the covenant in the presence of the LORD—to follow the LORD and keep his commands, statutes and decrees with all his heart and all his soul, thus confirming the words of the covenant written in this book.

2 KINGS 22:11–23:3

In May 2001, English evangelist J. John spoke in Liverpool, England, on the eighth commandment: "You shall not steal" (Exodus 20:15; Deuteronomy 5:19). The results of his preaching were dramatic.

People's hearts were changed. One author reported that large amounts of stolen goods were returned—including hotel towels, hospital crutches, library books, cash, and more. One man, who is now in the ministry, even returned towels he had taken from the venue of the Wimbledon tennis championships years earlier when he worked there.

Something similar happened with King Josiah in the eighteenth year of his reign. Because of the long line of evil kings, the record of God's laws had been lost. So when Hilkiah found God's law and Shaphan read it to King Josiah, the king tore his clothes in grief and immediately began making religious reforms in his own life and throughout the nation. With just one reading of God's Word, he changed the course of the nation (2 Kings 22:8–23:25).

Today, many of us own Bibles, but are we changed by the truths found there? We are called to read, hear, and obey His Word. It should cause us, like Josiah, to take immediate action to bring our lives into harmony with God's desires.

———

OPEN YOUR BIBLE PRAYERFULLY;
READ IT CAREFULLY.

*Therefore, my dear friends, as you have always obeyed—
not only in my presence, but now much more in my absence—
continue to work out your salvation with fear and trembling,
for it is God who works in you to will and to act in order to
fulfill his good purpose.*

*Do everything without grumbling or arguing, so that you
may become blameless and pure, "children of God without fault
in a warped and crooked generation." Then you will shine
among them like stars in the sky as you hold firmly to the word
of life. And then I will be able to boast on the day of Christ
that I did not run or labor in vain. But even if I am being
poured out like a drink offering on the sacrifice and service
coming from your faith, I am glad and rejoice with all of you.
So you too should be glad and rejoice with me.*

PHILIPPIANS 2:12–18

We always crave change in a new year. This is why on January 1 we start diets, exercise programs, and new hobbies. Of course, a month later we're usually back to our old bad habits. Maybe that's because we crave too big a change and do not have enough power and will to make the changes.

I wonder how many Jesus-followers made commitments to change and grow spiritually back in January as the calendar turned but are now experiencing frustration because they don't have the will and power to carry out those steps.

Paul addresses this issue in his letter to the Philippians. As he encouraged them to work out their salvation with fear and trembling (2:12), Paul said they would not be on their own. God himself would energize them to grow and carry out His tasks. The first area affected would be their desires. God was at work in them, giving them the desire to change and grow. He was also working to give them the power to make the actual changes (v. 13).

God has not left us alone in our struggles to attain spiritual growth. He helps us want to obey Him, and then He gives us the power to do what He wants. Ask Him to help you want to do His will.

———

THE POWER THAT COMPELS US COMES
FROM THE SPIRIT WHO INDWELLS US.

The church throughout Judea, Galilee and Samaria enjoyed a time of peace and was strengthened. Living in the fear of the Lord and encouraged by the Holy Spirit, it increased in numbers.

As Peter traveled about the country, he went to visit the Lord's people who lived in Lydda. There he found a man named Aeneas, who was paralyzed and had been bedridden for eight years. "Aeneas," Peter said to him, "Jesus Christ heals you. Get up and roll up your mat." Immediately Aeneas got up. All those who lived in Lydda and Sharon saw him and turned to the Lord.

In Joppa there was a disciple named Tabitha (in Greek her name is Dorcas); she was always doing good and helping the poor. About that time she became sick and died, and her body was washed and placed in an upstairs room. Lydda was near Joppa; so when the disciples heard that Peter was in Lydda, they sent two men to him and urged him, "Please come at once!"

Peter went with them, and when he arrived he was taken upstairs to the room. All the widows stood around him, crying and showing him the robes and other clothing that Dorcas had made while she was still with them.

Peter sent them all out of the room; then he got down on his knees and prayed. Turning toward the dead woman, he said, "Tabitha, get up." She opened her eyes, and seeing Peter she sat up. He took her by the hand and helped her to her feet. Then he called for the believers, especially the widows, and presented her to them alive.

ACTS 9:31–41

Dr. Martin Luther King once said: "The well-off and the secure have too often become indifferent and oblivious to the poverty and deprivation in their midst. The poor … have been shut out of our minds and driven from the mainstream of our societies, because we have allowed them to become invisible.… Ultimately, a great nation is a compassionate nation. No individual or nation can be great if it does not have a concern for 'the least of these.'"

In Joppa, Dorcas must have been viewed as a great person due to her concern for "the least of these." Luke uses a Greek word that means "female disciple" to describe her (v. 36). The term was a high honor for a woman, and it meant she was committed to pattern her life after Jesus's life.

This commitment was expressed through her beautiful works on behalf of the poor, especially the widows in Joppa (v. 39). Her selfless deeds toward the "least of these" flowed from her close relationship with Jesus (John 15:5). His life worked through her, and she actively sought to do what Jesus desired. Her compassionate deeds likely came out of her understanding that she was God's masterpiece, created in Christ to do good works (Ephesians 2:10). She desired to serve real people in real time, giving her life away to the poor.

Grace has appeared to us in Jesus. Our way of thanking Him is to break open our lives and pour out His love on the broken people around us.

———

WE ARE NOT SAVED BY GOOD WORKS
BUT FOR GOOD WORKS.

The wrath of God is being revealed from heaven against all the godlessness and wickedness of people, who suppress the truth by their wickedness, since what may be known about God is plain to them, because God has made it plain to them. For since the creation of the world God's invisible qualities— his eternal power and divine nature—have been clearly seen, being understood from what has been made, so that people are without excuse.

For although they knew God, they neither glorified him as God nor gave thanks to him, but their thinking became futile and their foolish hearts were darkened. Although they claimed to be wise, they became fools and exchanged the glory of the immortal God for images made to look like a mortal human being and birds and animals and reptiles.

ROMANS 1:18–23

A man wearing jeans, a T-shirt, and a baseball cap positioned himself against a wall beside a trash can at the L'Enfant Plaza Metro station in Washington, DC. He pulled out a violin and began to play. In the next forty-three minutes, as he performed six classical pieces, 1,097 people passed by, ignoring him.

No one knew it, but the man playing outside the Metro was Joshua Bell, one of the finest classical musicians in the world, playing some of the most elegant music ever written on a $3.5 million Stradivarius. But no crowd gathered for the virtuoso. "It was a strange feeling, that people were actually … ignoring me," said Bell.

God also knows what it feels like to be ignored. The apostle Paul said that God has sovereignly planted evidence of His existence in the very nature of man. And creation delivers an unmistakable message about His creativity, beauty, power, and character. Although God has revealed His majesty, many refuse to acknowledge and thank Him. But God will hold everyone responsible for ignoring who He is and what He has revealed: "People are without excuse. For although they knew God, they neither glorified him as God nor gave thanks to him" (Romans 1:20–21).

Let us acknowledge and thank the Virtuoso of heaven, who has wonderfully revealed himself to us.

ALL CREATION IS AN OUTSTRETCHED FINGER
POINTING TOWARD GOD.

Therefore if you have any encouragement from being united with Christ, if any comfort from his love, if any common sharing in the Spirit, if any tenderness and compassion, then make my joy complete by being like-minded, having the same love, being one in spirit and of one mind. Do nothing out of selfish ambition or vain conceit. Rather, in humility value others above yourselves, not looking to your own interests but each of you to the interests of the others.

In your relationships with one another, have the same mindset as Christ Jesus:

> *Who, being in very nature God, did not consider equality with God something to be used to his own advantage;*
> *rather, he made himself nothing by taking the very nature of a servant, being made in human likeness.*
> *And being found in appearance as a man, he humbled himself by becoming obedient to death—even death on a cross!*
>
> *Therefore God exalted him to the highest place and gave him the name that is above every name,*
> *that at the name of Jesus every knee should bow, in heaven and on earth and under the earth,*
> *and every tongue acknowledge that Jesus Christ is Lord, to the glory of God the Father.*

PHILIPPIANS 2:1–11

When was the last time you experienced conflict with a family member or friend? If you're like me, conflict between you and the people you love strips you of the full measure of Christian joy.

One of Paul's purposes in writing to the Philippians was to help them experience a full measure of joy—realized by reducing the friction in their relationships. He knew there was only one way this could happen. They would need to show one another the deep love God had shown them (2:2). This love was unconditional and nondiscriminating. It was a love for one another that should be growing, not eroding.

Next, they could reduce conflict by working together with one mind and purpose (v. 2). This did not mean they had to think and act alike. It meant they should be striving passionately for the same goal—the glory of God and His kingdom. Also, they could reduce conflict by having the right motivation for serving others and by celebrating the spiritual growth in the lives of fellow believers (v. 3). Paul charged them to extend their concern beyond themselves and to relinquish their fascination with personalities, especially their own (v. 4). His motivation for these strong commands was the most powerful example of unity and humility ever known—Jesus Christ (vv. 5–11).

As we interact with others, we will face conflict. But we can experience the full measure of joy as we continue to be motivated by the example of our Savior. Let's reduce conflict by living in unity and loving others with humility.

———

THE KEY TO GETTING ALONG WITH OTHERS
IS HAVING THE MIND OF CHRIST.

On one occasion an expert in the law stood up to test Jesus. "Teacher," he asked, "what must I do to inherit eternal life?"

"What is written in the Law?" he replied. "How do you read it?"

He answered, " 'Love the Lord your God with all your heart and with all your soul and with all your strength and with all your mind'; and, 'Love your neighbor as yourself.' "

"You have answered correctly," Jesus replied. "Do this and you will live."

But he wanted to justify himself, so he asked Jesus, "And who is my neighbor?"

In reply Jesus said: "A man was going down from Jerusalem to Jericho, when he was attacked by robbers. They stripped him of his clothes, beat him and went away, leaving him half dead. A priest happened to be going down the same road, and when he saw the man, he passed by on the other side. So too, a Levite, when he came to the place and saw him, passed by on the other side. But a Samaritan, as he traveled, came where the man was; and when he saw him, he took pity on him. He went to him and bandaged his wounds, pouring on oil and wine. Then he put the man on his own donkey, brought him to an inn and took care of him. The next day he took out two denarii and gave them to the innkeeper. 'Look after him,' he said, 'and when I return, I will reimburse you....'

"Which of these three do you think was a neighbor to the man who fell into the hands of robbers?"

The expert in the law replied, "The one who had mercy on him." Jesus told him, "Go and do likewise."

LUKE 10:25–37

One of the major obstacles to showing compassion is making prejudgments about who we think is worthy of our compassion. Jesus told a parable to answer the question: "Who is my neighbor?" (Luke 10:29). Or, who qualifies as worthy of our neighborly acts?

Jesus told of a man who traveled on the notoriously dangerous road from Jerusalem to Jericho. As he traveled, he fell among thieves and was robbed, beaten, and left for dead. Religious Jews (a priest and a Levite) passed him, but they walked by on the other side, probably for fear of being religiously defiled. But a Samaritan came along and had unconditional compassion on the wounded stranger.

Jesus's audience would have gasped at this because Jews despised Samaritans. The Samaritan could have limited or qualified his compassion because the man was a Jew. But he did not limit his neighborly kindness to those he thought were worthy. Instead, he saw a human being in need and resolved to help him.

Are you limiting your kindness to the ones you deem worthy? As followers of Jesus, let us find ways to show neighborly kindness to all people, especially to those we have judged as unworthy.

———

OUR LOVE FOR CHRIST IS ONLY AS REAL
AS OUR LOVE FOR OUR NEIGHBOR.

"Declare to my people their rebellion and to the descendants of Jacob their sins. For day after day they seek me out; they seem eager to know my ways, as if they were a nation that does what is right and has not forsaken the commands of its God. They ask me for just decisions and seem eager for God to come near them. 'Why have we fasted,' they say, 'and you have not seen it? Why have we humbled ourselves, and you have not noticed?'

"Yet on the day of your fasting, you do as you please and exploit all your workers. Your fasting ends in quarreling and strife, and in striking each other with wicked fists. You cannot fast as you do today and expect your voice to be heard on high....

"Is not this the kind of fasting I have chosen: to loose the chains of injustice and untie the cords of the yoke, to set the oppressed free and break every yoke? Is it not to share your food with the hungry and to provide the poor wanderer with shelter—when you see the naked, to clothe them, and not to turn away from your own flesh and blood?

"Then your light will break forth like the dawn, and your healing will quickly appear; then your righteousness will go before you, and the glory of the LORD will be your rear guard. Then you will call, and the LORD will answer; you will cry for help, and he will say: Here am I.

"If you do away with the yoke of oppression, with the pointing finger and malicious talk, and if you spend yourselves in behalf of the hungry and satisfy the needs of the oppressed, then your light will rise in the darkness, and your night will become like the noonday."

ISAIAH 58:1–10

In 1963, during a peaceful march on Washington, DC, Dr. Martin Luther King, delivered his now famous *I Have a Dream* speech. He eloquently called for freedom to ring from every mountaintop across the nation. The cost to him personally and to those who joined his peaceful resistance movement was steep, but real change soon began. God used that speech to awaken the conscience of the US to fight for the freedom of the oppressed and downtrodden.

In the eighth century BC, amid personal and national injustice, the prophet Isaiah was used by God to awaken the conscience of His people. Their convenient spirituality had led them to violence and insensitivity toward their fellow humans. God's people were oppressing the poor and substituting religious practices for genuine righteous living (vv. 1–5). God indicted them (v. 1) and prescribed spiritual living that would be expressed through turning to God in genuine repentance and setting people free (vv. 6–12).

Like Isaiah, we have been sent to let freedom ring. By the power of the Holy Spirit, we must proclaim that the captives can be released, that the downtrodden can be freed from their oppressors, and that the time of the Lord's favor has come.

———

NO RIGHTEOUSNESS,
NO FREEDOM!

"The rest of the people—priests, Levites, gatekeepers, musicians, temple servants and all who separated themselves from the neighboring peoples for the sake of the Law of God, together with their wives and all their sons and daughters who are able to understand—all these now join their fellow Israelites the nobles, and bind themselves with a curse and an oath to follow the Law of God given through Moses the servant of God and to obey carefully all the commands, regulations and decrees of the LORD our Lord.

"We promise not to give our daughters in marriage to the peoples around us or take their daughters for our sons.

"When the neighboring peoples bring merchandise or grain to sell on the Sabbath, we will not buy from them on the Sabbath or on any holy day. Every seventh year we will forgo working the land and will cancel all debts."

NEHEMIAH 10:28–31

In 1722, Jonathan Edwards drew up a list of seventy resolutions, dedicating himself to live in harmony with God and others. The following resolutions give a picture of the serious purpose with which Edwards approached his relationship with God. He resolved:

- To do whatever is most to God's glory.
- To do my duty, for the good of mankind in general.
- Never to do anything, which I should be afraid to do, if it were the last hour of my life.
- To study the Scriptures steadily, constantly, and frequently.
- To ask myself at the end of every day, week, month, and year if I could possibly have done better.
- Until I die, not to act as if I were my own, but entirely and altogether God's.

In Nehemiah 10, God's people made an oath, vowing to follow all the commands, laws, and regulations of the Lord. This oath was so serious that they were willing to accept the curse of God if they failed to keep these commands.

Our resolutions need not be as serious as that. But any resolution to follow God is not a casual promise. Rather, it is a solemn and serious declaration that—with the help of the Holy Spirit—we can renew every day.

―――――

ACT ON YOUR RESOLUTIONS!

"*You have heard that it was said to the people long ago, 'You shall not murder, and anyone who murders will be subject to judgment.' But I tell you that anyone who is angry with a brother or sister will be subject to judgment. Again, anyone who says to a brother or sister, 'Raca,' is answerable to the court. And anyone who says, 'You fool!' will be in danger of the fire of hell.*

"*Therefore, if you are offering your gift at the altar and there remember that your brother or sister has something against you, leave your gift there in front of the altar. First go and be reconciled to them; then come and offer your gift.*

"*Settle matters quickly with your adversary who is taking you to court. Do it while you are still together on the way, or your adversary may hand you over to the judge, and the judge may hand you over to the officer, and you may be thrown into prison. Truly I tell you, you will not get out until you have paid the last penny.*"

MATTHEW 5:21–26

Several years ago, when he was in college, Jesse Jacobs created an apology hotline. This hotline made it possible for people to apologize without actually talking to the person they wronged. People who were unable or unwilling to unburden their conscience in person called the hotline and left a message on an answering machine. Each week, thirty to fifty calls were logged as people apologized for things from adultery to embezzlement. "The hotline offers participants a chance to alleviate their guilt and, to some degree, to own up to their misdeeds," said Jacobs at the time.

The apology hotline may seem to offer some relief from guilt, but this is not how Jesus instructed His followers to handle conflict. In the Sermon on the Mount, Jesus told us to deal with conflict by taking the initiative and going to the offended brother to apologize for the offense (see also Matthew 18). In fact, Jesus taught that the problem of human estrangement is so serious that we should even interrupt our worship to go on a personal mission of reconciliation (Matthew 5:24). The Master encouraged His followers to be reconciled with one another eagerly, aggressively, quickly, and personally (v. 25).

Are any of your relationships broken or estranged because of something you said or did? Take the initiative. Go now and do all you can to be reconciled.

———

AT THE HEART OF ALL CONFLICT
IS A SELFISH HEART.

Now Ahab told Jezebel everything Elijah had done and how he had killed all the prophets with the sword. So Jezebel sent a messenger to Elijah to say, "May the gods deal with me, be it ever so severely, if by this time tomorrow I do not make your life like that of one of them."

Elijah was afraid and ran for his life.... He came to a broom bush, sat down under it and prayed that he might die. "I have had enough, Lord," he said. "Take my life; I am no better than my ancestors." Then he lay down under the bush and fell asleep.

All at once an angel touched him and said, "Get up and eat." He looked around, and there by his head was some bread baked over hot coals, and a jar of water. He ate and drank and then lay down again.

The angel of the Lord came back a second time and touched him and said, "Get up and eat, for the journey is too much for you." So he got up and ate and drank. Strengthened by that food, he traveled forty days and forty nights until he reached Horeb, the mountain of God. There he went into a cave and spent the night.

And the word of the Lord came to him: "What are you doing here, Elijah?"

He replied, "I have been very zealous for the Lord God Almighty. The Israelites have rejected your covenant, torn down your altars, and put your prophets to death with the sword. I am the only one left, and now they are trying to kill me too."

The Lord said, "Go out and stand on the mountain in the presence of the Lord, for the Lord is about to pass by."

1 KINGS 19:1–11

Almost everyone will at some time in life be affected by depression, either his or her own or someone else's. Some common signs and symptoms of depression include feelings of hopelessness, pessimism, worthlessness, and helplessness. Although we cannot say for certain that characters in the Bible experienced depression, we can say that some did exhibit a deep sense of despondency, discouragement, and sadness that is linked to personal powerlessness and loss of meaning and enthusiasm for life.

Elijah is one biblical character who fits this description. After defeating the prophets of Baal, he received a death threat from Jezebel. His hope was shattered, and despondency set in. He wanted to die! God helped Elijah deal with his despondency in several ways. The Lord did not rebuke him for his feelings but sent an angel to provide for his physical needs. Then the Lord revealed himself and reminded Elijah that He was quietly working among His people. Next, He renewed Elijah's mission by giving him new orders. Finally, God reminded Elijah that he wasn't alone.

In our times of discouragement, let us remember that God loves us and desires to lead us to a place of a renewed vision of himself!

————

THE WEAK, THE HELPLESS,
AND THE DISCOURAGED
ARE IN THE SHEPHERD'S SPECIAL CARE.

"No one can come to me unless the Father who sent me draws them, and I will raise them up at the last day. It is written in the Prophets: 'They will all be taught by God.' Everyone who has heard the Father and learned from him comes to me. No one has seen the Father except the one who is from God; only he has seen the Father. Very truly I tell you, the one who believes has eternal life. I am the bread of life. Your ancestors ate the manna in the wilderness, yet they died. But here is the bread that comes down from heaven, which anyone may eat and not die. I am the living bread that came down from heaven. Whoever eats this bread will live forever. This bread is my flesh, which I will give for the life of the world."

Then the Jews began to argue sharply among themselves, "How can this man give us his flesh to eat?"

Jesus said to them, "Very truly I tell you, unless you eat the flesh of the Son of Man and drink his blood, you have no life in you. Whoever eats my flesh and drinks my blood has eternal life, and I will raise them up at the last day. For my flesh is real food and my blood is real drink. Whoever eats my flesh and drinks my blood remains in me, and I in them. Just as the living Father sent me and I live because of the Father, so the one who feeds on me will live because of me. This is the bread that came down from heaven. Your ancestors ate manna and died, but whoever feeds on this bread will live forever."

JOHN 6:44–58

A few years ago, a company advertised a "huggable, washable, and talking" Jesus doll that recited "actual Scripture verses to introduce children of all ages to the wisdom of the Bible." Its sayings included, "I have an exciting plan for your life," and "Your life matters so much to Me." Who wouldn't want to follow a Jesus like this?

Jesus does offer a wonderful plan for our lives. But He doesn't serve as a cosmic genie or cuddly doll to meet our every whim. John 6 gives us a picture of a Jesus who is not so cuddly; in fact, He's often offensive. Instead of fulfilling the selfish desires of His followers, He disturbed their expectations. He offered himself as spiritual bread from heaven and explained this symbolically by saying, "Whoever eats my flesh and drinks my blood has eternal life" (v. 54).

This message was offensive and difficult. The image of eating flesh and drinking blood did not give His hearers "warm fuzzies." Many stopped following Him (v. 66). He wasn't the conquering Messiah-King they had expected.

Sometimes we want a Jesus who meets our selfish needs. But the wonderful life He offers is found only in radical obedience to His commands. Let's ask Jesus to show us what His words mean and to give us the courage to act on His truth.

THE WAY OF JESUS IS NOT
ALWAYS EASY.

The LORD said to Moses, "Say to the Israelites: 'Any man or woman who wrongs another in any way and so is unfaithful to the LORD is guilty and must confess the sin they have committed. They must make full restitution for the wrong they have done, add a fifth of the value to it and give it all to the person they have wronged. But if that person has no close relative to whom restitution can be made for the wrong, the restitution belongs to the LORD and must be given to the priest, along with the ram with which atonement is made for the wrongdoer.'"

NUMBERS 5:5–8

Researchers at the University of Toronto reported that people who are suffering from a guilty conscience experience "a powerful urge to wash themselves." To study this effect, the researchers asked volunteers to recall past sins. They were then given an opportunity to wash their hands as a symbol of cleansing their conscience. Those who had recalled their sins washed their hands at "twice the rate of study subjects who had not imagined past transgressions."

The Bible proposes the only effective way of dealing with sin—confession. In the Old Testament, one of the ways the Israelites were supposed to cleanse themselves and maintain purity before God and in their community was by confessing their sins (Numbers 5:5–8). *To confess* means "to speak the same; to agree with; to admit the truth." When the people confessed to God, they were not telling Him anything He did not already know. But their confession was a demonstration of a changed heart. Refusing to confess their sins allowed sin to take deeper root within their lives and community.

Admitting our sin unlocks the gate so we can have forgiveness, joy, and peace. If we confess our sins, God is faithful to forgive (1 John 1:9).

———

CONFESSION IS AGREEING
WITH GOD ABOUT OUR SIN.

Uzziah was sixteen years old when he became king, and he reigned in Jerusalem fifty-two years. His mother's name was Jekoliah; she was from Jerusalem. He did what was right in the eyes of the LORD, just as his father Amaziah had done. He sought God during the days of Zechariah, who instructed him in the fear of God. As long as he sought the LORD, God gave him success.

He went to war against the Philistines and broke down the walls of Gath, Jabneh and Ashdod ... and his fame spread as far as the border of Egypt, because he had become very powerful....

But after Uzziah became powerful, his pride led to his downfall. He was unfaithful to the LORD his God, and entered the temple of the LORD to burn incense on the altar of incense. Azariah the priest with eighty other courageous priests of the LORD followed him in. They confronted King Uzziah and said, "It is not right for you, Uzziah, to burn incense to the LORD ..."

Uzziah, who had a censer in his hand ready to burn incense, became angry. While he was raging at the priests in their presence before the incense altar in the LORD's temple, leprosy broke out on his forehead. When Azariah the chief priest and all the other priests looked at him, they saw that he had leprosy on his forehead, so they hurried him out. Indeed, he himself was eager to leave, because the LORD had afflicted him.

King Uzziah had leprosy until the day he died. He lived in a separate house—leprous, and banned from the temple of the LORD.

2 CHRONICLES 26:1–21

Evangelist D. L. Moody once said, "When a man thinks he has a good deal of strength, and is self-confident, you may look for his downfall. It may be years before it comes to light, but it is already commenced." This was definitely true of King Uzziah.

Everything seemed to be going so well in the monarch's life. He lived in covenant obedience to the Lord, and he sought God's guidance during most of his reign. As long as he asked God for guidance and help, God gave him great success. His success was evidenced by his many accomplishments (2 Chronicles 26:2, 7–15). But then he was blinded by his power and success, which caused him to be filled with pride.

Uzziah's pride was evidenced in several ways: He challenged God's holiness by trespassing into the temple (v. 16); he viewed God's power as nice but not absolutely necessary (vv. 5, 16); when confronted with his pride, he refused godly correction and counsel; he refused to repent, and he ignored—instead of feared—the consequences of his sin (vv. 18–19). Uzziah's pride motivated him to glorify himself and contend for God's supremacy. What a tragic ending to a promising life!

The story of Uzziah teaches us several key lessons: View God's help as absolutely necessary, remember the Source of all our blessings, thank God for those blessings, and accept godly and worthwhile counsel. May we choose, as William Penn says, a "low and level dwelling!" For God opposes the proud but gives grace to the humble (James 4:6).

———

HUMILITY PROMOTES UNITY.

Slaves, obey your earthly masters in everything; and do it, not only when their eye is on you and to curry their favor, but with sincerity of heart and reverence for the Lord.

Whatever you do, work at it with all your heart, as working for the Lord, not for human masters, since you know that you will receive an inheritance from the Lord as a reward. It is the Lord Christ you are serving. Anyone who does wrong will be repaid for their wrongs, and there is no favoritism. Masters, provide your slaves with what is right and fair, because you know that you also have a Master in heaven.

COLOSSIANS 3:22–4:1

Spencer Johnson, author of *Who Moved My Cheese?* stated: "Research may one day show that the only long-lasting motivation will come from employees who bring it to work in the form of God, spirituality, or something else that causes them to rise to a higher purpose." Long before Dr. Johnson, the apostle Paul said that slaves (employees) and masters (employers) should be motivated by a higher purpose in their jobs—their relationship with Jesus.

In Colossians 3:22–4:1, Paul discussed three important aspects of work—*mandate*, *manner*, and *motivation*. Employees have the *mandate* to obey their bosses out of reverence for Christ (3:22). The *manner* in which they obey flows from a sincere heart and with a right attitude (v. 23). Employees can overcome the lack of *motivation* in their work by focusing on their true motivation: working for Jesus (v. 24).

Paul also addressed employers, who should treat their employees with fairness and justice as they honor their Master in heaven (4:1; Philemon 16).

As followers of Jesus who work in the marketplace, we're called to rise to a higher purpose in our jobs. If we are employees, unless we know a task is sinful, we should do the job we were hired to do with excellence and the right attitude. If we are employers, we should create fair and just environments out of our reverence and love for Jesus.

In both roles, we're missionaries on assignment—representing the Master.

———

BE THE WORK GREAT OR SMALL;
DO IT WELL OR NOT AT ALL.

GUESS WHO'S COMING TO DINNER

Jesus replied: "A certain man was preparing a great banquet and invited many guests. At the time of the banquet he sent his servant to tell those who had been invited, 'Come, for everything is now ready.'

"But they all alike began to make excuses. The first said, 'I have just bought a field, and I must go and see it. Please excuse me.'

"Another said, 'I have just bought five yoke of oxen, and I'm on my way to try them out. Please excuse me.'

"Still another said, 'I just got married, so I can't come.'

"The servant came back and reported this to his master. Then the owner of the house became angry and ordered his servant, 'Go out quickly into the streets and alleys of the town and bring in the poor, the crippled, the blind and the lame.'

"'Sir,' the servant said, 'what you ordered has been done, but there is still room.'

"Then the master told his servant, 'Go out to the roads and country lanes and compel them to come in, so that my house will be full. I tell you, not one of those who were invited will get a taste of my banquet.'"

LUKE 14:16–24

Several times a year, I receive dinner invitations to partner with various organizations. Some of these invitations spark no interest in me, while others are so close to my heart that I respond with an enthusiastic, "Yes!"

Jesus once used an illustration to talk about a dinner invitation that deserved a hearty "yes" from everyone. In Luke 14, a wealthy man sent out invitations to a dinner party. To get such a personal invitation was a distinct honor. When the dinner was ready, he sent his servant to notify the guests (v. 17). That's when the unthinkable happened.

His guests showed no respect for his invitation. They made excuses why they could not attend (vv. 18–20). You'd think the host would cancel the dinner, but he didn't. He sent out *more* invitations (v. 21). He sent his servant to invite the unwanted, the unfit, and the unworthy of society to the feast, until the tables were full of guests (v. 23).

This brief but important story reveals a wonderful truth about God: He values *all* of humanity—particularly the less fortunate. Moreover, this story reveals a truth about the gospel. The message of salvation is an invitation to everyone, but it is especially good news to those who struggle.

How can we live this out? By passionately, unconditionally, and extravagantly loving everyone—especially the marginalized in our world. Let's invite them all to the wonderful feast of God's love.

———

TRUE CHRISTIAN LOVE HELPS THOSE
WHO CAN'T RETURN THE FAVOR.

Not that I have already obtained all this, or have already arrived at my goal, but I press on to take hold of that for which Christ Jesus took hold of me. Brothers and sisters, I do not consider myself yet to have taken hold of it. But one thing I do: Forgetting what is behind and straining toward what is ahead, I press on toward the goal to win the prize for which God has called me heavenward in Christ Jesus.

All of us, then, who are mature should take such a view of things. And if on some point you think differently, that too God will make clear to you. Only let us live up to what we have already attained.

Join together in following my example, brothers and sisters, and just as you have us as a model, keep your eyes on those who live as we do. For, as I have often told you before and now tell you again even with tears, many live as enemies of the cross of Christ. Their destiny is destruction, their god is their stomach, and their glory is in their shame. Their mind is set on earthly things. But our citizenship is in heaven. And we eagerly await a Savior from there, the Lord Jesus Christ, who, by the power that enables him to bring everything under his control, will transform our lowly bodies so that they will be like his glorious body.

PHILIPPIANS 3:12–21

One of my favorite television programs is *The Amazing Race*. This reality show takes up to a dozen couples (people in pre-existing relationships) and places them in a foreign country where they race—via trains, buses, cabs, bikes, and feet—from one point to the next, gaining instructions for the next challenge. The goal is to get to the designated finishing point before everyone else. The last couple to make it to each finishing point is eliminated. And the pair who wins the race receives one million dollars.

Paul said that he was in a race too. He admitted that he had not fully developed as a Christian and that there was room for improvement in his walk with Jesus (Philippians 3:12). He was in a race, making progress, racing toward the finish line of being conformed to the image of Jesus and having perfect fellowship with Him forever. As he ran the race, he didn't look back, but he moved forward despite his failures because he knew that Jesus had forgiven him (v. 13).

As believers in Jesus, we're also running a race. We're in process, striving to make progress in our spiritual life. If we want to constantly grow in Christ, we must also forget the past and focus on the future. We can move forward despite our failures, knowing that we have been forgiven.

We're racing, not for a million dollars, but for the ultimate prize of being more like Jesus. Let's "press on to reach the end of the race" (v. 14).

———

THE FAITH THAT CONTINUES TO THE END
GIVES PROOF THAT IT WAS GENUINE
IN THE BEGINNING.

Therefore hear the word of the LORD, you scoffers who rule this people in Jerusalem. You boast, "We have entered into a covenant with death, with the realm of the dead we have made an agreement. When an overwhelming scourge sweeps by, it cannot touch us, for we have made a lie our refuge and falsehood our hiding place."

So this is what the Sovereign LORD says: "See, I lay a stone in Zion, a tested stone, a precious cornerstone for a sure foundation, the one who relies on it will never be stricken with panic. I will make justice the measuring line and righteousness the plumb line; hail will sweep away your refuge, the lie, and water will overflow your hiding place. Your covenant with death will be annulled; your agreement with the realm of the dead will not stand. When the overwhelming scourge sweeps by, you will be beaten down by it. As often as it comes it will carry you away; morning after morning, by day and by night, it will sweep through."

The understanding of this message will bring sheer terror. The bed is too short to stretch out on, the blanket too narrow to wrap around you. The LORD will rise up as he did at Mount Perazim, he will rouse himself as in the Valley of Gibeon—to do his work, his strange work, and perform his task, his alien task. Now stop your mocking, or your chains will become heavier; the Lord, the LORD Almighty, has told me of the destruction decreed against the whole land.

ISAIAH 28:14–22

During a leaders' gathering, my friend Chad watched intensely as his daughter, Hannah, climbed a rock wall. Hannah was making progress, until she began slipping a bit. Chad called out to her, "Put your feet on the rock!" He wanted his daughter to find stability. Isaiah had the same idea in mind when prophesying about the coming Messiah in Isaiah 28. The prophet described Him as the rock on which God's people should place their feet (v. 16). In what ways is Jesus like a rock? Check these out:

- The stone was tested. As a foundation stone, it had been carefully inspected to determine its strength. What's more, this "cornerstone" was prepared by the master mason to be placed at the start of the building process—determining the course of the entire structure (Psalm 118:22; Mark 12:10). The Messiah would be the perfect One—the perfect fit—for God's plan of salvation (Mark 12:6), and a proven foundation for those who believe in Him.

- The stone was Messiah Jesus. He lived a perfect life; and He was crucified, buried, and raised from the dead. He alone can save and provide a firm foundation in life. Faith in Him is what makes the difference during unstable and difficult times. He's been tested and proven, and His strength can handle the weight of our sin and struggles.

Let's stand on the Rock—Jesus Christ.

THE WISE PERSON BUILDS
HIS HOUSE ON THE ROCK.
—Jesus

*But the Israelites were unfaithful in regard to the devoted things; Achan … took some of them. So the L*ORD*'s anger burned against Israel.*

Now Joshua sent men from Jericho to Ai, which is near Beth Aven to the east of Bethel, and told them, "Go up and spy out the region.…"

When they returned to Joshua, they said, "Not all the army will have to go up against Ai. Send two or three thousand men to take it and do not weary the whole army, for only a few people live there." So about three thousand went up; but they were routed by the men of Ai.…

*Then Joshua tore his clothes and fell facedown to the ground before the ark of the L*ORD*, remaining there till evening. The elders of Israel did the same, and sprinkled dust on their heads. And Joshua said, "Alas, Sovereign L*ORD*, why did you ever bring this people across the Jordan to deliver us into the hands of the Amorites to destroy us?… What can I say, now that Israel has been routed by its enemies?…"*

*The L*ORD *said to Joshua, "Stand up! What are you doing down on your face? Israel has sinned; they have violated my covenant, which I commanded them to keep. They have taken some of the devoted things;… That is why the Israelites cannot stand against their enemies.…*

*"Go, consecrate the people. Tell them, 'Consecrate yourselves in preparation for tomorrow; for this is what the L*ORD*, the God of Israel, says: There are devoted things among you, Israel. You cannot stand against your enemies until you remove them.*

"'In the morning, present yourselves tribe by tribe.…'"

Early the next morning Joshua had Israel come forward by tribes, …

*Then Joshua said to Achan, "My son, give glory to the L*ORD*, the God of Israel, and honor him. Tell me what you have done; do not hide it from me."*

JOSHUA 7:1–19

100

One of the dangers of past success is that it can lead to complacency. Positive outcomes are exciting, but they can make us feel overconfident. Soon we may be humbled and brought back to reality if we experience failure.

This seems to be what Joshua and Israel felt when they went to take Ai (Joshua 7:2–3). God had given them overwhelming victory in their previous battle at Jericho. They must have thought taking Ai would be a piece of cake. They were wrong (vv. 4–5).

What happened? They were crushed because a guy named Achan had clandestinely breached the covenant by coveting and taking the devoted things (v. 1). As a result, the Lord's anger burned against the whole community of Israel.

God pointed out to Joshua that Israel had violated His covenant, and He instructed him to deal severely with the perpetrator. Joshua obeyed God. Achan confessed his failure, and he and his entire family were punished.

Achan's sad story teaches us: (1) Sin will weaken God's people. (2) Sin always has consequences. (3) When we fail, we need to refocus on God and His glory. (4) We should confess our sins to God and others. (5) When we deal with sin, we must eradicate it. (6) Spiritual failure teaches us not to make the same mistake twice (Joshua 8:1). By God's grace, we can move on.

———

INSTEAD OF LIVING IN THE SHADOWS OF
YESTERDAY, WALK IN THE LIGHT OF TODAY
AND THE HOPE OF TOMORROW.

Then God said, "Let us make mankind in our image, in our likeness, so that they may rule over the fish in the sea and the birds in the sky, over the livestock and all the wild animals, and over all the creatures that move along the ground."

So God created mankind in his own image,
     in the image of God he created them;
     male and female he created them.

God blessed them and said to them, "Be fruitful and increase in number; fill the earth and subdue it. Rule over the fish in the sea and the birds in the sky and over every living creature that moves on the ground."

Then God said, "I give you every seed-bearing plant on the face of the whole earth and every tree that has fruit with seed in it. They will be yours for food. And to all the beasts of the earth and all the birds in the sky and all the creatures that move along the ground—everything that has the breath of life in it—I give every green plant for food." And it was so.

God saw all that he had made, and it was very good. And there was evening, and there was morning—the sixth day.

Thus the heavens and the earth were completed in all their vast array.

By the seventh day God had finished the work he had been doing; so on the seventh day he rested … from all the work of creating that he had done.

GENESIS 1:26–2:3

Michelangelo was an Italian sculptor, architect, and poet whose artistic accomplishments exerted a tremendous influence on his contemporaries and on subsequent European art. The sad reality is, however, that he left many of his works unfinished.

Whether or not all His creatures realize it, God, the divine sculptor and architect of the universe, finished His works (Genesis 2:1–2). Having finished creating the world, He evaluated it and said it was good (1:31). Then He rested—not because He was weary, but because creation was finished.

Not only did God complete His creation but in Jesus He also finished the work of redemption. As He was nearing the end of His earthly work, Jesus explained that His nourishment came from doing the will of God and finishing His work (John 4:34). And He did just that! While on the cross, Jesus cried out, "It is finished" (John 19:30). Access to an authentic relationship with God was made available through His sacrificial death.

As believers in Jesus, we're called to finish our God-ordained assignments (Colossians 4:17)—telling others the good news of God's love and grace.

Let's finish the work assigned to us so we can say, like the apostle Paul, "I have fought the good fight, I have finished the race, I have kept the faith" (2 Timothy 4:7).

———

SUCCESS IS NOT JUDGED BY HOW WE START
BUT BY WHAT WE FINISH.

David again brought together all the able young men of Israel—thirty thousand. He and all his men went to Baalah in Judah to bring up from there the ark of God.... They set the ark of God on a new cart and brought it from the house of Abinadab, which was on the hill. Uzzah and Ahio, sons of Abinadab, were guiding the new cart with the ark of God on it, and Ahio was walking in front of it....

When they came to the threshing floor of Nakon, Uzzah reached out and took hold of the ark of God, because the oxen stumbled. The LORD's anger burned against Uzzah because of his irreverent act; therefore God struck him down, and he died there beside the ark of God.

Then David was angry because the LORD's wrath had broken out against Uzzah, and to this day that place is called Perez Uzzah.

David was afraid of the LORD that day and said, "How can the ark of the LORD ever come to me?" He was not willing to take the ark of the LORD to be with him in the City of David. Instead, he took it to the house of Obed-Edom the Gittite. The ark of the LORD remained in the house of Obed-Edom the Gittite for three months, and the LORD blessed him and his entire household.

2 SAMUEL 6:1–11

To my own embarrassment, I must admit that there have been times when I've taken my wife for granted. After a couple of decades of marriage, I've been so familiar with her presence that I've been insensitive to her needs and wants.

Just as it's not healthy to take our spouses for granted, King David would say it's not healthy to take God for granted. Desiring to unite the nation spiritually, David went to retrieve the ark of the covenant from Kiriath-Jearim, where it had been located for over twenty-five years. His men transported the ark on a new cart (2 Samuel 6:3). But as they transported the precious piece, the oxen stumbled, and a man named Uzzah reached out—with good intentions—to stabilize the ark. When he touched it, God's judgment broke out against him and he died (v. 7).

David became angry and afraid of God, and he decided to abandon the mission (v. 10). Could it be that God had responded with such drastic measures because David had taken Him for granted? David assumed he knew what God would approve. In this failure, David had begun to trifle with God's holiness and standards (Numbers 4:15, 20; Deuteronomy 10:8).

This narrative reveals how God feels about placing our preferences ahead of His purposes. And it reminds us that obedience to God's specific will is more important than good intentions.

May we approach God with awe and according to His revealed will! Serve the Lord with reverent fear, and rejoice with trembling (Psalm 2:11).

———

TRUE WORSHIP GIVES
GOD CENTER STAGE.

*When you enter the land the L*ORD *your God is giving you, do not learn to imitate the detestable ways of the nations there. Let no one be found among you who sacrifices their son or daughter in the fire, who practices divination or sorcery, interprets omens, engages in witchcraft, or casts spells, or who is a medium or spiritist or who consults the dead. Anyone who does these things is detestable to the L*ORD*; because of these same detestable practices the L*ORD *your God will drive out those nations before you. You must be blameless before the L*ORD *your God.*

*The nations you will dispossess listen to those who practice sorcery or divination. But as for you, the L*ORD *your God has not permitted you to do so.*

DEUTERONOMY 18:9–14

There's a growing fascination today with life after death. Thousands of so-called psychics claim to contact the spirits of the dead. And online, people can visit with psychics, spirit guides, and experts in reincarnation. There are nearly 13,000 reincarnation sites, 12,000 psychics sites, and more than 1,000 sites dedicated to talking with the dead.

God told Moses to warn Israel that deliberate involvement with contacting the deceased was forbidden (Leviticus 19:31; Deuteronomy 18:9–14). Talking to mediums, seeking spirits, practicing sorcery and divination to try to contact the dead were forbidden because these practices prevented Israel from being a peculiar people—a people who would be a blessing to all nations (Leviticus 20:6–8). How could she influence her neighbors if she was imitating their evil behavior?

So, why did people attempt to contact the dead? They were:

- desperate for guidance (1 Samuel 28:3–15)
- disobedient to God (1 Chronicles 10:13–14)
- deceived (2 Corinthians 2:10–11; 11:3)

For believers, these practices are forbidden as well. These practices are the fruit of the sin nature (Galatians 5:19–21). Believers who seek help in contacting the dead are choosing to follow Satan.

Instead of having a fascination with contacting the dead, we should initiate loving contact with the living. That way we can tell them about God who—through His Son—loves them and can secure their eternal life.

***

THOSE WHO FEAR GOD
NEED NOT FEAR DEATH.

Therefore, as God's chosen people, holy and dearly loved, clothe yourselves with compassion, kindness, humility, gentleness and patience. Bear with each other and forgive one another if any of you has a grievance against someone. Forgive as the Lord forgave you. And over all these virtues put on love, which binds them all together in perfect unity.

Let the peace of Christ rule in your hearts, since as members of one body you were called to peace. And be thankful. Let the message of Christ dwell among you richly as you teach and admonish one another with all wisdom through psalms, hymns, and songs from the Spirit, singing to God with gratitude in your hearts. And whatever you do, whether in word or deed, do it all in the name of the Lord Jesus, giving thanks to God the Father through him.

COLOSSIANS 3:12–17

During winter in my part of the world, we don't often get warm, sunny days. Recently, God blessed us with one of those days. As I left the office to go home, a man said, "What a wonderful day! This is a gift from God." I replied, "Yeah, but there's going to be a major snowstorm later this week." Oops. What an ugly display of ingratitude! To change my ways, I'm on a quest to build a life and theology of thanksgiving. The apostle Paul, in his letters, is helping me get there.

Paul mentioned thanksgiving in his letters more often—line for line—than any other Greek author (pagan or Christian). Here are a few lessons he taught us about thanksgiving:

1. *Thanksgiving should be primarily directed to God.* Paul gave thanks to God for growth, love, faith, risks, and receiving and accepting the Word (Romans 16:4; 1 Corinthians 1:4; 1 Thessalonians 1:2).

2. *Thanksgiving should be given unceasingly.* He regularly carved out time to make sure thanksgiving played a key role in his prayer life (Colossians 3:15).

3. *Thanksgiving flows from a heart changed by God.* Grace, God's favor and salvation through Jesus, leads to the response, "God, thank You" (vv. 12–15).

4. *Thanksgiving is given through Jesus, for everything* (Ephesians 5:20; Colossians 3:15, 17).

5. *Thanksgiving is an important part of praise, worship, and glorifying God* (2 Corinthians 4:15–17).

Let's ask God to help us realize all He's done for us—and then respond with gratitude.

———

WE DON'T NEED MORE TO BE THANKFUL FOR;
WE NEED TO BE MORE THANKFUL.

The vision of Obadiah. This is what the Sovereign LORD
says about Edom—We have heard a message from the LORD:
An envoy was sent to the nations to say, "Rise, let us go against
her for battle"—

"See, I will make you small among the nations; you will be
utterly despised. The pride of your heart has deceived you,
you who live in the clefts of the rocks and make your home on
the heights, you who say to yourself, 'Who can bring me down
to the ground?' Though you soar like the eagle and make your
nest among the stars, from there I will bring you down," declares
the LORD. "If thieves came to you, if robbers in the night, oh,
what a disaster awaits you!—would they not steal only as much
as they wanted? If grape pickers came to you, would they not
leave a few grapes? But how Esau will be ransacked, his hidden
treasures pillaged! All your allies will force you to the border;
your friends will deceive and overpower you; those who eat your
bread will set a trap for you, but you will not detect it.

"In that day," declares the LORD, "will I not destroy the
wise men of Edom, those of understanding in the mountains of
Esau? Your warriors, Teman, will be terrified, and everyone in
Esau's mountains will be cut down in the slaughter. Because of
the violence against your brother Jacob, you will be covered with
shame; you will be destroyed forever. On the day you stood aloof
while strangers carried off his wealth and foreigners entered his
gates and cast lots for Jerusalem, you were like one of them. You
should not gloat over your brother in the day of his misfortune.

OBADIAH 1:1–12

Years ago, Charles Haddon Spurgeon wrote in *Sermons on Sovereignty*: "There are two sins of man that are bred in the bone, and that continually come out in the flesh. One is self-dependence and the other is self-exaltation."

Hundreds of years after Esau and Jacob's birthday, God expressed His holy anger and condemnation toward the Edomites' pride (Obadiah 1:1–2). They had attacked the Judeans during the Babylonian crisis, instead of assisting them (vv. 10–14). They delighted in bringing disaster to God's people. This greatly displeased God. He also condemned their pride of heart that made them think they were indestructible (v. 3).

The Edomites lived in a mountainous region with elevations up to 5,000 feet above sea level. Their inaccessible location had given them a false sense of security. The sins of self-dependence and self-exaltation were bred in their bones and were continually coming out in their words and actions. Edom asked, "Who can ever reach us way up here?" The Lord answered: "I will bring you crashing down" (v. 4 NLT).

God still opposes the proud and arrogant. Every human effort at self-security will ultimately fail and be made small before God. What God desires from His people is humility —an attitude of submission and obedience, grounded in the acknowledgment of our true needy status before Him.

TRUE HUMILITY IS NOT
LOOKING DOWN ON YOURSELF,
BUT LOOKING UP AT GOD.

Thanks be to God, who delivers me through Jesus Christ our Lord!

So then, I myself in my mind am a slave to God's law, but in my sinful nature a slave to the law of sin.

Therefore, there is now no condemnation for those who are in Christ Jesus.

ROMANS 7:25–8:1

The Thirteenth Amendment, which abolished slavery in the United States, was ratified on December 6, 1865. So, how many slaves were there in the US on December 7?

Technically, there were none. However, there were many who did not know about the amendment and continued to live like slaves. And there were others who knew they were free but doubted the reality of their freedom.

This seems to be true of many believers in Jesus today. An "amendment of freedom" has been passed by the death of Jesus, but many doubt the reality of their freedom and continue to live like slaves to sin.

This is what Paul spoke of in Romans 8, which begins with "Therefore," a word that referred to the earlier themes of Romans: freedom from sin, justification by faith alone, friendship with God, and assurance of salvation and eternal life—all achieved through Christ.

Paul reminded his readers, "There is now no condemnation for those who are in Christ Jesus" (v. 1). In this verse, Paul communicated that we're no longer condemned under the penalty of sin, and there's no condemnation or peril that could ever separate us from the love of Christ (vv. 31–39).

Sin and failure can cause us to doubt the reality of the freedom Jesus provided. He alone has secured and sustained our salvation. It's all about Him, not our performance.

———

THERE IS NO CONDEMNATION
FOR THOSE WHO BELONG
TO CHRIST JESUS.

113

Who is wise and understanding among you? Let them show it by their good life, by deeds done in the humility that comes from wisdom. But if you harbor bitter envy and selfish ambition in your hearts, do not boast about it or deny the truth. Such "wisdom" does not come down from heaven but is earthly, unspiritual, demonic. For where you have envy and selfish ambition, there you find disorder and every evil practice.

But the wisdom that comes from heaven is first of all pure; then peace-loving, considerate, submissive, full of mercy and good fruit, impartial and sincere. Peacemakers who sow in peace reap a harvest of righteousness.

JAMES 3:13–18

James, the brother of Jesus, was one of the most prominent leaders in the early church. Under the power of the Holy Spirit, he demonstrated his writing skills and uncommon wisdom when he penned five chapters in the greatest book in the world—the Bible. In chapter three, James defined two types of wisdom—spiritual and godly; unspiritual and ungodly. According to verses 14–16, being bitterly jealous and selfish is the epitome of being unwise. James's readers would have understood what his words meant: Having ill will toward others, creating cliques, measuring yourself by your own standards, and denying what God says about you are all characteristics of an ungodly and a devil-motivated wisdom.

In verses 17–18, James presents some characteristics of godly wisdom: walking in integrity with God and others (purity); refusing to awaken and incite anger in other people (peace loving, planting seeds of peace); valuing and accepting other people's feelings, opinions, and suggestions (gentle, yielding to others); forgiving others' mistakes and sins (merciful); and being transparent about my weaknesses (sincerity).

Jesus is the wisdom of God (1 Corinthians 1:30). When we stay connected to Him (John 15:5), His values and very life will be formed in us and His wisdom—from above—will flow through us.

———

TRUE WISDOM
BEGINS AND ENDS
WITH GOD.

"I am the true vine, and my Father is the gardener. He cuts off every branch in me that bears no fruit, while every branch that does bear fruit he prunes so that it will be even more fruitful. You are already clean because of the word I have spoken to you. Remain in me, as I also remain in you. No branch can bear fruit by itself; it must remain in the vine. Neither can you bear fruit unless you remain in me.

"I am the vine; you are the branches. If you remain in me and I in you, you will bear much fruit; apart from me you can do nothing. If you do not remain in me, you are like a branch that is thrown away and withers; such branches are picked up, thrown into the fire and burned. If you remain in me and my words remain in you, ask whatever you wish, and it will be done for you. This is to my Father's glory, that you bear much fruit, showing yourselves to be my disciples.

"As the Father has loved me, so have I loved you. Now remain in my love. If you keep my commands, you will remain in my love, just as I have kept my Father's commands and remain in his love. I have told you this so that my joy may be in you and that your joy may be complete. My command is this: Love each other as I have loved you. Greater love has no one than this: to lay down one's life for one's friends."

JOHN 15:1–13

How is behavior altered? In his book *The Social Animal*, David Brooks notes that some experts have said people just need to be taught the long-term risks of bad behavior. For example, he writes: "Smoking can lead to cancer. Adultery destroys families, and lying destroys trust. The assumption was that once you reminded people of the foolishness of their behavior, they would be motivated to stop. Both reason and will are obviously important in making moral decisions and exercising self-control. But neither of these character models has proven very effective." In other words, information alone is not powerful enough to transform behavior.

As Jesus's followers, we want to grow and change spiritually. More than two millennia ago, Jesus told His disciples how that can happen. He said, "Remain in me, as I also remain in you. No branch can bear fruit by itself, it must remain in the vine. Neither can you bear fruit unless you remain in me" (John 15:4). Jesus is the Vine and we, His followers, are the branches. If we're honest, we know we're utterly helpless and spiritually ineffective apart from Him.

Jesus transforms us spiritually and reproduces His life in us—as we abide in Him.

———

A CHANGE IN BEHAVIOR BEGINS
WITH JESUS CHANGING OUR HEART.

Do not take advantage of a hired worker who is poor and needy, whether that worker is a fellow Israelite or a foreigner residing in one of your towns. Pay them their wages each day before sunset, because they are poor and are counting on it. Otherwise they may cry to the LORD against you, and you will be guilty of sin.

Parents are not to be put to death for their children, nor children put to death for their parents; each will die for their own sin.

Do not deprive the foreigner or the fatherless of justice, or take the cloak of the widow as a pledge. Remember that you were slaves in Egypt and the LORD your God redeemed you from there. That is why I command you to do this.

When you are harvesting in your field and you overlook a sheaf, do not go back to get it. Leave it for the foreigner, the fatherless and the widow, so that the LORD your God may bless you in all the work of your hands. When you beat the olives from your trees, do not go over the branches a second time. Leave what remains for the foreigner, the fatherless and the widow. When you harvest the grapes in your vineyard, do not go over the vines again. Leave what remains for the foreigner, the fatherless and the widow. Remember that you were slaves in Egypt. That is why I command you to do this.

DEUTERONOMY 24:14–22

When Presbyterian clergyman Elijah Lovejoy (1802–1837) left the pulpit, he returned to the printing presses in order to reach more people. After witnessing a lynching, Lovejoy committed to fighting the injustice of slavery. His life was threatened by hateful mobs, but this did not stop him: "If by compromise is meant that I should cease from my duty, I cannot make it. I fear God more than I fear man. Crush me if you will, but I shall die at my post." Four days after these words, he was killed at the hands of another angry mob.

Concern about justice for the oppressed is evident throughout Scripture. It was especially clear when God established the rules for His covenant people after they were released from Egyptian bondage (Deuteronomy 24:18–22). Moses emphasized concern for the underprivileged (Exodus 22:22–27; 23:6–9; Leviticus 19:9–10). Repeatedly, the Israelites were reminded that they had been slaves in Egypt and should deal justly with the underprivileged in their community. They were to love strangers ("foreigners") because God loves them, and the Israelites had themselves been foreigners in Egypt (Exodus 23:9; Leviticus 19:34; Deuteronomy 10:17–19).

God desires that His people affirm the supreme worth of every individual by fighting against injustice.

———

STANDING FOR JUSTICE
MEANS FIGHTING AGAINST INJUSTICE.

Some Hebrews even crossed the Jordan to the land of Gad and Gilead.

Saul remained at Gilgal, and all the troops with him were quaking with fear. He waited seven days, the time set by Samuel; but Samuel did not come to Gilgal, and Saul's men began to scatter. So he said, "Bring me the burnt offering and the fellowship offerings." And Saul offered up the burnt offering. Just as he finished making the offering, Samuel arrived, and Saul went out to greet him.

"What have you done?" asked Samuel.

Saul replied, "When I saw that the men were scattering, and that you did not come at the set time, and that the Philistines were assembling at Mikmash, I thought, 'Now the Philistines will come down against me at Gilgal, and I have not sought the LORD's favor.' So I felt compelled to offer the burnt offering."

"You have done a foolish thing," Samuel said. "You have not kept the command the LORD your God gave you; if you had, he would have established your kingdom over Israel for all time. But now your kingdom will not endure; the LORD has sought out a man after his own heart and appointed him ruler of his people, because you have not kept the LORD's command."

1 SAMUEL 13:7–14

In an act of impatience, a man in San Francisco, California, tried to beat traffic by swerving around a lane of cars that had come to a stop. However, the lane he pulled into had just been laid with fresh cement, and his Porsche 911 got stuck. This driver paid a high price for his impatience.

The Scriptures tell of a king who also paid a high price for his impatience. Eager for God to bless the Israelites in their battle against the Philistines, Saul acted impatiently. When Samuel did not arrive at the appointed time to offer a sacrifice for God's favor, Saul became impatient and disobeyed God's command (1 Samuel 13:8–9, 13). Impatience led Saul to think he was above the law and to take on an unauthorized position of priest. He thought he could disobey God without serious consequences. He was wrong.

When Samuel arrived, he rebuked Saul for his disobedience and prophesied that Saul would lose the kingdom (vv. 13–14). Saul's refusal to wait for the development of God's plan caused him to act in haste, and in his haste he lost his way (see Proverbs 19:2). His impatience was the ultimate display of a lack of faith.

The Lord will provide His guiding presence as we wait patiently for Him to bring about His will.

———

PATIENCE MEANS AWAITING GOD'S TIME
AND TRUSTING GOD'S LOVE.

When he noticed how the guests picked the places of honor at the table, he told them this parable: "When someone invites you to a wedding feast, do not take the place of honor, for a person more distinguished than you may have been invited. If so, the host who invited both of you will come and say to you, 'Give this person your seat.' Then, humiliated, you will have to take the least important place. But when you are invited, take the lowest place, so that when your host comes, he will say to you, 'Friend, move up to a better place.' Then you will be honored in the presence of all the other guests. For all those who exalt themselves will be humbled, and those who humble themselves will be exalted."

Then Jesus said to his host, "When you give a luncheon or dinner, do not invite your friends, your brothers or sisters, your relatives, or your rich neighbors; if you do, they may invite you back and so you will be repaid. But when you give a banquet, invite the poor, the crippled, the lame, the blind, and you will be blessed. Although they cannot repay you, you will be repaid at the resurrection of the righteous."

LUKE 14:7–14

I love hosting festive dinners. Sometimes I'll say: "Tonia, we haven't had anyone over for dinner in a while. Who do you think we should invite?" We go through our proposed guest list and suggest friends we have never invited or have not invited in a while. And it seems like this list is normally comprised of people who look and sound and live like we do, and who can reciprocate. But if we were to ask Jesus whom we should have over for dinner, He would give us a totally different guest list.

One day a prominent Pharisee invited Jesus into his home, probably for table fellowship, but possibly to watch Him closely so he could trap Him. While there, Jesus healed a man and taught the host a significant lesson: When making out your guest list for a dinner party, you should not be exclusive—inviting friends, relatives, rich neighbors, and those who can pay you back. Instead, you should be inclusive—inviting the poor, the crippled, the lame, and the blind. Although such people would not be able to pay the host back, Jesus assured him that he would be blessed and that God would reward him (Luke 14:12–14).

Just as Jesus loves the less fortunate, He invites us to love them by opening up our hearts and homes.

———

OPENING OUR HEARTS AND HOMES
BLESSES BOTH US AND OTHERS.

Therefore each of you must put off falsehood and speak truthfully to your neighbor, for we are all members of one body. "In your anger do not sin": Do not let the sun go down while you are still angry, and do not give the devil a foothold. Anyone who has been stealing must steal no longer, but must work, doing something useful with their own hands, that they may have something to share with those in need.

Do not let any unwholesome talk come out of your mouths, but only what is helpful for building others up according to their needs, that it may benefit those who listen. And do not grieve the Holy Spirit of God, with whom you were sealed for the day of redemption. Get rid of all bitterness, rage and anger, brawling and slander, along with every form of malice. Be kind and compassionate to one another, forgiving each other, just as in Christ God forgave you.

EPHESIANS 4:25–32

A while back, an Emmy Award-winning actress took a courageous stand and walked out in the middle of the annual American Music Awards ceremony. Her reason? She grew increasingly upset and disappointed by what she described as "an onslaught of lewd jokes and off-color remarks" and raw and raunchy comments by presenters, performers, and hosts. She said the evening was an affront to anyone with a shred of dignity and self-respect.

Unwholesome speech was a problem even in the apostle Paul's day. He reminded the Christians at Ephesus that they should put away vulgarity, lewdness, slander, and obscene talk from their lives (Ephesians 5:4; Colossians 3:8). These were expressions of their old lives (1 Corinthians 6:9–11), and it was now out of place with their new identity in Christ. Instead, their lives were to be characterized by wholesome speech. Their good or wholesome words would give grace to the hearers (Ephesians 4:29). The Holy Spirit would help guard their speech, convict of any filthy talk, and help them to use words to benefit others (John 16:7–13).

We are called to reflect God with all we are, and that includes our words. May our mouths be filled with thanksgiving and words that benefit others.

———

WHOLESOME WORDS FLOW OUT
OF A LIFE MADE NEW.

Giving joyful thanks to the Father, who has qualified you to share in the inheritance of his holy people in the kingdom of light. For he has rescued us from the dominion of darkness and brought us into the kingdom of the Son he loves, in whom we have redemption, the forgiveness of sins.

The Son is the image of the invisible God, the firstborn over all creation. For in him all things were created: things in heaven and on earth, visible and invisible, whether thrones or powers or rulers or authorities; all things have been created through him and for him. He is before all things, and in him all things hold together. And he is the head of the body, the church; he is the beginning and the firstborn from among the dead, so that in everything he might have the supremacy. For God was pleased to have all his fullness dwell in him, and through him to reconcile to himself all things, whether things on earth or things in heaven, by making peace through his blood, shed on the cross.

Once you were alienated from God and were enemies in your minds because of your evil behavior. But now he has reconciled you by Christ's physical body through death to present you holy in his sight, without blemish and free from accusation.

COLOSSIANS 1:12–22

A South African man surprised nine men robbing his home. Seven of the robbers ran away, but the homeowner managed to shove two into his backyard pool. After realizing that one of the robbers couldn't swim, the homeowner jumped in to save him. The *Cape Times* reports that once out of the pool, the wet thief called to his friends to come back. Then he pulled a knife and threatened the man who had just rescued him. The homeowner said, "We were still standing near the pool, and when I saw the knife I just threw him back in. But he was gasping for air and was drowning. So I rescued him again."

In his letter to the Colossians, the apostle Paul wrote of another rescue: God the Father had saved them from the domain of darkness. This rescue occurred at the death of Christ, but also at the Colossians' conversion. The imagery Paul used (1:12–13) suggests that believers have been rescued from the dark reign of Satan by being transferred as free people into the peaceable rule of Christ. By Jesus's death, believers become free citizens in the kingdom of light.

The appropriate response to such amazing grace is to show joyous gratitude by offering God acceptable service with reverence and awe (Hebrews 12:28).

———

THROUGH THE CROSS, JESUS RESCUED AND
REDEEMED THE REBELLIOUS.

For when we came into Macedonia, we had no rest, but we were harassed at every turn—conflicts on the outside, fears within. But God, who comforts the downcast, comforted us by the coming of Titus, and not only by his coming but also by the comfort you had given him. He told us about your longing for me, your deep sorrow, your ardent concern for me, so that my joy was greater than ever.

Even if I caused you sorrow by my letter, I do not regret it. Though I did regret it—I see that my letter hurt you, but only for a little while—yet now I am happy, not because you were made sorry, but because your sorrow led you to repentance. For you became sorrowful as God intended and so were not harmed in any way by us. Godly sorrow brings repentance that leads to salvation and leaves no regret, but worldly sorrow brings death.

2 CORINTHIANS 7:5–10

Thieves stole nearly $5,000 in sound and office equipment from a church in West Virginia, only to break in the following night to return the items they had taken. Apparently, the guilt of stealing from a church weighed so heavily on their conscience that they felt the need to correct their criminal behavior of breaking the commandment: "You shall not steal" (Exodus 20:15). Their actions make me think about the differences between worldly sorrow and godly sorrow.

Paul praised the Corinthians for understanding this difference. His first letter to them was biting, as he addressed issues of sin. His words caused sorrow among them, and because of this Paul rejoiced. Why? Their sorrow did not stop at just feeling sad about getting caught or suffering the unpleasant consequences of their sins. Their sorrow was godly sorrow, a genuine remorse for their sins. This led them to repentance—a change in their thinking that led to a renouncing of their sin and turning to God. Their repentance ultimately led to deliverance from their sinful habits.

Repenting is not something we can do unless we have the prompting of the Holy Spirit; it's a gift from God. Pray for repentance today (2 Timothy 2:24–26).

REPENTANCE MEANS HATING SIN
ENOUGH TO TURN FROM IT.

"Where were you when I laid the earth's foundation? Tell me, if you understand. Who marked off its dimensions? Surely you know! Who stretched a measuring line across it? On what were its footings set, or who laid its cornerstone—while the morning stars sang together and all the angels shouted for joy?

"Who shut up the sea behind doors when it burst forth from the womb, when I made the clouds its garment and wrapped it in thick darkness, when I fixed limits for it and set its doors and bars in place, when I said, 'This far you may come and no farther; here is where your proud waves halt'?

"Have you ever given orders to the morning, or shown the dawn its place, that it might take the earth by the edges and shake the wicked out of it? The earth takes shape like clay under a seal; its features stand out like those of a garment. The wicked are denied their light, and their upraised arm is broken.

"Have you journeyed to the springs of the sea or walked in the recesses of the deep? Have the gates of death been shown to you? Have you seen the gates of the deepest darkness? Have you comprehended the vast expanses of the earth? Tell me, if you know all this."

JOB 38:4–18

Willard S. Boyle, Nobel Prize winner in physics, was the co-inventor of the "electronic eye" behind the digital camera and the Hubble telescope. While in the market for a new digital camera, he visited a store in Halifax, Nova Scotia. The salesman tried to explain the complexity of the camera to Boyle, but he stopped because he felt it was too complicated for Boyle to understand. Boyle then bluntly said to the salesman: "No need to explain. I invented it."

After God allowed Satan to test Job by taking away his family, his health, and his possessions (Job 1–2), Job lamented the day of his birth (chapter 3). In the following chapters, Job questioned why God would allow him to endure so much suffering. Then with divine bluntness, God reminded Job that He "invented" life and created the world (see chapters 38–41). God invited him to rethink what he had said. In drawing attention to His sovereign power and the depth of His wisdom displayed everywhere on earth (38:4–41), God exposed the immensity of Job's ignorance. If we're tempted to tell God how life should work, let's remember this: He invented it! May He help us to humbly acknowledge our ignorance and to rely on Him—the Creator of the universe.

————

TO UNDERSTAND GOD IS IMPOSSIBLE,
BUT TO WORSHIP HIM IS IMPERATIVE.

In reply Jesus said: "A man was going down from Jerusalem to Jericho, when he was attacked by robbers. They stripped him of his clothes, beat him and went away, leaving him half dead. A priest happened to be going down the same road, and when he saw the man, he passed by on the other side. So too, a Levite, when he came to the place and saw him, passed by on the other side. But a Samaritan, as he traveled, came where the man was; and when he saw him, he took pity on him. He went to him and bandaged his wounds, pouring on oil and wine. Then he put the man on his own donkey, brought him to an inn and took care of him. The next day he took out two denarii and gave them to the innkeeper. 'Look after him,' he said, 'and when I return, I will reimburse you for any extra expense you may have.'

"Which of these three do you think was a neighbor to the man who fell into the hands of robbers?"

The expert in the law replied, "The one who had mercy on him."

Jesus told him, "Go and do likewise."

LUKE 10:30–37

Dr. Scott Kurtzman, chief of surgery at Waterbury Hospital in Connecticut, was on his way to deliver a lecture when he witnessed a horrible crash involving twenty vehicles. The doctor shifted into trauma mode, worked his way through the mess of metal, and called out, "Who needs help?" After ninety minutes of assisting, and after the victims had been taken to area hospitals, Dr. Kurtzman commented, "A person with my skills simply can't drive by someone who is injured. I refuse to live my life that way."

Jesus told a parable about a man who stopped to help another (Luke 10:30–37). A Jewish man had been ambushed, stripped, robbed, and left for dead. A Jewish priest and a temple assistant passed by, saw the man, and crossed over to the other side. Then a despised Samaritan came by, saw the man, and was filled with compassion. His compassion was translated into action: He soothed and bandaged the man's wounds, took him to an inn, cared for him while he could, paid for all his medical expenses, and then promised the innkeeper he would return to pay any additional expenses.

There are people around us who are suffering. Moved with compassion for their pain, let's be those who stop to help.

———

COMPASSION
IS ALWAYS ACTIVE.

How long, LORD? Will you forget me forever?
    How long will you hide your face from me?
How long must I wrestle with my thoughts
    and day after day have sorrow in my heart?
    How long will my enemy triumph over me?

Look on me and answer, LORD my God.
    Give light to my eyes, or I will sleep in death,
and my enemy will say, "I have overcome him,"
    and my foes will rejoice when I fall.

But I trust in your unfailing love;
    my heart rejoices in your salvation.
I will sing the LORD's praise,
    for he has been good to me.

PSALM 13

As Karissa Smith was browsing in a local library with her babbling four-month-old daughter, an older man rudely told her to quiet her baby or he would. Smith responded, "I am very sorry for whatever in your life caused you to be so disturbed by a happy baby, but I will not tell my baby to shut up, and I will not let you do so either." The man put his head down and apologized, and he told her the story of how his son died of Sudden Infant Death Syndrome over 50 years ago. He had repressed his grief and anger all those years.

In Psalm 13, David expressed his grief. He addressed God with raw and honest language: "How long, Lord? Will you forget me forever? How long will you hide your face from me?" (v. 1). These questions reflected fear of abandonment. David's language of distress gave way to a plea for help and reaffirmation of his faith in God's love for him (vv. 3–6). Confidence and firm resolve came alongside the cry of distress.

We all go through dark nights of the soul when we wonder if God has abandoned us. As with David, our aching can give way to joy when we approach God honestly, plead for help, and reaffirm our trust in Him. God's love for us will never waver or change.

———

GOD WILL NEVER LEAVE US
NOR FORSAKE US.

As for you, you were dead in your transgressions and sins, in which you used to live when you followed the ways of this world and of the ruler of the kingdom of the air, the spirit who is now at work in those who are disobedient. All of us also lived among them at one time, gratifying the cravings of our flesh and following its desires and thoughts. Like the rest, we were by nature deserving of wrath. But because of his great love for us, God, who is rich in mercy, made us alive with Christ even when we were dead in transgressions—it is by grace you have been saved. And God raised us up with Christ and seated us with him in the heavenly realms in Christ Jesus, in order that in the coming ages he might show the incomparable riches of his grace, expressed in his kindness to us in Christ Jesus. For it is by grace you have been saved, through faith—and this is not from yourselves, it is the gift of God—not by works, so that no one can boast. For we are God's handiwork, created in Christ Jesus to do good works, which God prepared in advance for us to do.

EPHESIANS 2:1–10

The Grand Rapids Art Museum has over 5,000 works of art, including 3,500 prints, drawings, and photographs; 1,000 works of design; and 700 paintings and sculptures. As I read about this museum and anticipated visiting it, I couldn't help but think about God's "museum."

God is an artist, and His creation is unspeakably magnificent. But it is not His greatest work! God's greatest work is His redemption of us. When we were still dead in our sins, He made us alive in His Son, Jesus Christ (Ephesians 2:1, 5). Paul reminded the Ephesians that they were God's "workmanship," or *poiema* (v. 10), a Greek term that means "poem" or "work of art." God's art museum is the church, filled with millions of marvelous works—His people.

Being God's work of art, Paul said, should result in something from us. We are not supposed to sit silently in the museum of fellowship. Rather, we are to show God's love in practical ways through our good works. Jesus said these good works glorify our heavenly Father (Matthew 5:16).

God did not re-create us in His Son to be museum pieces. He redeemed us so that our good works would showcase the brilliant colors of His redemption and grace, and draw a world in darkness to the light of His love.

THEY WITNESS BEST
WHO WITNESS WITH THEIR LIVES.

*Eli's sons were scoundrels; they had no regard for the
LORD... Now a man of God came to Eli and said to him,
"This is what the LORD says: 'Did I not clearly reveal myself to
your ancestor's family when they were in Egypt under Pharaoh?
I chose your ancestor out of all the tribes of Israel to be my
priest, to go up to my altar, to burn incense, and to wear an
ephod in my presence. I also gave your ancestor's family all the
food offerings presented by the Israelites. Why do you scorn my
sacrifice and offering that I prescribed for my dwelling? Why do
you honor your sons more than me by fattening yourselves on
the choice parts of every offering made by my people Israel?'*

*"Therefore the LORD, the God of Israel, declares: 'I
promised that members of your family would minister before
me forever.' But now the LORD declares: 'Far be it from me!
Those who honor me I will honor, but those who despise me
will be disdained. The time is coming when I will cut short
your strength and the strength of your priestly house, so that
no one in it will reach old age, and you will see distress in my
dwelling....*

*"'And what happens to your two sons, Hophni and
Phinehas, will be a sign to you—they will both die on the
same day. I will raise up for myself a faithful priest, who will
do according to what is in my heart and mind. I will firmly
establish his priestly house, and they will minister before my
anointed one always. Then everyone left in your family line will
come and bow down before him ...'"*

1 SAMUEL 2:12, 27–36

Therapist and mother Lori Gottlieb says that parents who are obsessed with their children's happiness may actually contribute to their becoming unhappy adults. These parents coddle their children, do not equip them to deal with the real world, look the other way when their children do wrong, and neglect disciplining them.

In 1 Samuel, we read that the high priest Eli sometimes looked the other way. We don't know what he was like as a father when his boys were young. But he failed to properly deal with their behavior as grown men serving in God's temple. They were selfish, lustful, and rebellious, putting their own needs ahead of God's Word and the needs of the people. At first, Eli rebuked them, but they would not listen. Instead of removing them from service, he looked the other way and let them continue in their sin. As a result of his sons' sins and because Eli honored his sons above the Lord (1 Samuel 2:29), the Lord warned Eli that his family would suffer judgment (v. 34; 4:17–18).

As Christian parents, we have the awesome responsibility to lovingly discipline our children (Proverbs 13:24; 29:17; Hebrews 12:9–11). As we impart God's wisdom to them, we have the blessing of helping them develop into responsible, God-fearing adults.

FAILURE TO DISCIPLINE OUR CHILDREN
IS A FAILURE TO LOVE THEM.

Make every effort to live in peace with everyone and to be holy; without holiness no one will see the Lord. See to it that no one falls short of the grace of God and that no bitter root grows up to cause trouble and defile many. See that no one is sexually immoral, or is godless like Esau, who for a single meal sold his inheritance rights as the oldest son. Afterward, as you know, when he wanted to inherit this blessing, he was rejected. Even though he sought the blessing with tears, he could not change what he had done.

You have not come to a mountain that can be touched and that is burning with fire; to darkness, gloom and storm; to a trumpet blast or to such a voice speaking words that those who heard it begged that no further word be spoken to them, because they could not bear what was commanded: "If even an animal touches the mountain, it must be stoned to death." The sight was so terrifying that Moses said, "I am trembling with fear."

But you have come to Mount Zion, to the city of the living God, the heavenly Jerusalem. You have come to thousands upon thousands of angels in joyful assembly, to the church of the firstborn, whose names are written in heaven. You have come to God, the Judge of all, to the spirits of the righteous made perfect, to Jesus the mediator of a new covenant, and to the sprinkled blood that speaks a better word than the blood of Abel.

See to it that you do not refuse him who speaks. If they did not escape when they refused him who warned them on earth, how much less will we, if we turn away from him who warns us from heaven?

HEBREWS 12:14–25

In June 1966, Rubin "Hurricane" Carter, a celebrated boxer at the time—along with an acquaintance—was convicted of murder in a highly publicized and racially charged trial. The prize-fighter maintained his innocence and became his own jailhouse lawyer. After serving nineteen years, Carter was released when the verdict was overturned. As a free man, he reflected: "Wouldn't anyone under those circumstances have a right to be bitter? … I've learned that bitterness only consumes the vessel that contains it. And for me to permit bitterness to control or infect my life in any way whatsoever would be to allow those who imprisoned me to take even more than … they've already taken."

I believe bitterness is what the writer of Hebrews had in mind when he penned his warnings in chapter 12. In today's text, some of the Christians may have been considering returning to Judaism because of persecution and injustice. Like a small root that grows into a great tree, bitterness could spring up in their hearts and overshadow their deepest Christian relationships (12:15).

When we hold on to disappointment, a poisonous root of bitterness begins to grow. Let's allow the Spirit to fill us so He can heal the hurt that causes bitterness.

———

BITTERNESS IS A ROOT
THAT RUINS THE GARDEN OF PEACE.

"For the eyes of the Lord are on the righteous
    and his ears are attentive to their prayer,
but the face of the Lord is against those who do evil."

Who is going to harm you if you are eager to do good? But even if you should suffer for what is right, you are blessed. "Do not fear their threats; do not be frightened." But in your hearts revere Christ as Lord. Always be prepared to give an answer to everyone who asks you to give the reason for the hope that you have. But do this with gentleness and respect, keeping a clear conscience, so that those who speak maliciously against your good behavior in Christ may be ashamed of their slander. For it is better, if it is God's will, to suffer for doing good than for doing evil. For Christ also suffered once for sins, the righteous for the unrighteous, to bring you to God. He was put to death in the body but made alive in the Spirit. After being made alive, he went and made proclamation to the imprisoned spirits— to those who were disobedient long ago when God waited patiently in the days of Noah while the ark was being built. In it only a few people, eight in all, were saved through water, and this water symbolizes baptism that now saves you also—not the removal of dirt from the body but the pledge of a clear conscience toward God. It saves you by the resurrection of Jesus Christ, who has gone into heaven and is at God's right hand— with angels, authorities and powers in submission to him.

1 PETER 3:12–22

Lee Eclov and his wife were at a coffee shop in Estes Park, Colorado. At another table sat four men, one of whom was mocking Christianity and the resurrection of Jesus.

Lee could sense the Lord telling him to respond. But his fear kept him from doing so. Finally, he knew he had to make a stand. So he walked over to the men and began giving historical evidence for the resurrection.

How do we respond when we're in a similar situation? The apostle Peter encouraged his readers to make a commitment to stand up for Jesus, especially during extreme suffering. This commitment meant not remaining speechless when circumstances warranted them to defend their faith. He said, "Always be prepared to give an answer to everyone who asks you to give the reason for the hope that you have. But do this with gentleness and respect" (1 Peter 3:15–16). Their readiness to answer required them to know God's Word. They were to respond in godly gentleness and respect, so that their persecutors would be ashamed of their own conduct.

Had Lee Eclov remained silent or responded rudely, the cause of Christ would have suffered. Lee later wrote, "God has a way of flushing us out of our quiet little places and when He does, we must be ready to speak for Him."

———

TO BE SILENT ABOUT THE SAVIOR
AND HIS SALVATION
IS A DREADFUL SIN OF OMISSION.

After this, Paul left Athens and went to Corinth. There he met a Jew named Aquila, a native of Pontus, who had recently come from Italy with his wife Priscilla, because Claudius had ordered all Jews to leave Rome. Paul went to see them, and because he was a tentmaker as they were, he stayed and worked with them. Every Sabbath he reasoned in the synagogue, trying to persuade Jews and Greeks.

ACTS 18:1–4

In *Outlive Your Life*, Max Lucado writes: "Hospitality opens the door to uncommon community. It's no accident that hospitality and hospital come from the same Latin word, for they both lead to the same result: healing. When you open your door to someone, you are sending this message: 'You matter to me and to God.' You may think you are saying, 'Come over for a visit.' But what your guest hears is, 'I'm worth the effort.'"

This is what the apostle Paul must have heard and felt when Aquila and Priscilla opened the doors of their home to him. When he arrived in Corinth, he was probably exhausted from his journey from Athens. He may also have been discouraged because of his seemingly unsuccessful ministry there (Acts 17:16–34). He later wrote, "I came to you in weakness with fear and great trembling" (1 Corinthians 2:3). Aquila and Priscilla probably met Paul in the marketplace of Corinth and opened their home to him. They provided a spiritual oasis through Christian hospitality.

As followers of Jesus, we are called to be hospitable, to be a "hospital" that helps those who are going through life's storms and need restoration. We can be used by the Lord because He has provided for us.

———

CHRISTIAN HOSPITALITY IS AN OPEN HEART
AND AN OPEN HOME.

Saul replied, "You are not able to go out against this Philistine and fight him; you are only a young man, and he has been a warrior from his youth."

But David said to Saul, "... The LORD who rescued me from the paw of the lion and the paw of the bear will rescue me from the hand of this Philistine."

Saul said to David, "Go, and the LORD be with you." ...

Meanwhile, the Philistine, with his shield bearer in front of him, kept coming closer to David. He looked David over and saw that he was little more than a boy, glowing with health and handsome, and he despised him. He said to David, "Am I a dog, that you come at me with sticks?" ...

David said to the Philistine, "You come against me with sword and spear and javelin, but I come against you in the name of the LORD Almighty, the God of the armies of Israel, whom you have defied. This day the LORD will deliver you into my hands, and I'll strike you down and cut off your head.... All those gathered here will know that it is not by sword or spear that the LORD saves; for the battle is the LORD's, and he will give all of you into our hands."

As the Philistine moved closer to attack him, David ran quickly toward the battle line to meet him. Reaching into his bag and taking out a stone, he slung it and struck the Philistine on the forehead. The stone sank into his forehead, and he fell facedown on the ground.

So David triumphed over the Philistine with a sling and a stone; without a sword in his hand he struck down the Philistine and killed him.

1 SAMUEL 17:33–50

In 1935, the debate team of Wiley College, a small and unranked black school in Texas, unexpectedly defeated the all-white championship team from the University of Southern California. This was a classic case of the unknown triumphing over a national giant.

When ancient Israel was in peril at the hands of the Philistines, there was a boy named David who actually triumphed over a giant (1 Samuel 17). The armies were drawn up on opposite sides of the Valley of Elah. They were probably afraid of one another and decided that the outcome of the battle should be determined by a battle of champions. The Philistines offered Goliath, a giant (about 9' 9"), but Israel could not find anyone who was worthy or brave enough to fight. David heard of the dilemma and appealed to Saul to let him fight Goliath (vv. 32–37). Saul was reluctant, but he agreed. David, armed with five smooth stones (v. 40) and unswerving faith in the Almighty God (v. 45), triumphed over the Philistines' national champion.

We all face giants in our lives—worry, doubt, fear, sin, and guilt. But with limited and unlikely resources and unswerving confidence in our all-powerful God, we too can triumph over them.

———

GOD GIVES US COURAGE
TO CHALLENGE OUR GIANTS.

The Lord is my shepherd, I lack nothing.
   He makes me lie down in green pastures,
he leads me beside quiet waters,
   he refreshes my soul.
He guides me along the right paths
   for his name's sake.
Even though I walk
   through the darkest valley,
I will fear no evil,
   for you are with me;
your rod and your staff,
   they comfort me.

You prepare a table before me
   in the presence of my enemies.
You anoint my head with oil;
   my cup overflows.
Surely your goodness and love will follow me
   all the days of my life,
and I will dwell in the house of the Lord
   forever.

                              PSALM 23

In his classic book *A Shepherd Looks at Psalm 23*, W. Phillip Keller gives a striking picture of the care and gentleness of a shepherd. In verse 3 when David says, "He restores my soul," he uses language every shepherd would understand.

Sheep are built in such a way that if they fall over on their side and then onto their back, it is very difficult for them to get up again. They flail their legs in the air, bleat, and cry. After a few hours on their backs, gas begins to collect in their stomachs, the stomach hardens, the air passage is cut off, and the sheep will eventually suffocate. This is referred to as a "cast down" position.

When a shepherd restores a cast-down sheep, he reassures it, massages its legs to restore circulation, gently turns the sheep over, lifts it up, and holds it so it can regain its equilibrium.

What a picture of what God wants to do for us! When we are on our backs, flailing because of guilt, grief, or grudges, our loving Shepherd reassures us with His grace, lifts us up, and holds us until we've gained our spiritual equilibrium.

If you've been cast down for any reason, God is the only one who can help you get on your feet again. He will restore your confidence, joy, and strength.

———

THE WEAK AND THE HELPLESS ARE
IN THE GOOD SHEPHERD'S SPECIAL CARE.

When Cephas came to Antioch, I opposed him to his face, because he stood condemned. For before certain men came from James, he used to eat with the Gentiles. But when they arrived, he began to draw back and separate himself from the Gentiles because he was afraid of those who belonged to the circumcision group. The other Jews joined him in his hypocrisy, so that by their hypocrisy even Barnabas was led astray.

When I saw that they were not acting in line with the truth of the gospel, I said to Cephas in front of them all, "You are a Jew, yet you live like a Gentile and not like a Jew. How is it, then, that you force Gentiles to follow Jewish customs?

"We who are Jews by birth and not sinful Gentiles know that a person is not justified by the works of the law, but by faith in Jesus Christ. So we, too, have put our faith in Christ Jesus that we may be justified by faith in Christ and not by the works of the law, because by the works of the law no one will be justified.

"But if, in seeking to be justified in Christ, we Jews find ourselves also among the sinners, doesn't that mean that Christ promotes sin? Absolutely not! If I rebuild what I destroyed, then I really would be a lawbreaker.

"For through the law I died to the law so that I might live for God. I have been crucified with Christ and I no longer live, but Christ lives in me. The life I now live in the body, I live by faith in the Son of God, who loved me and gave himself for me. I do not set aside the grace of God, for if righteousness could be gained through the law, Christ died for nothing!"

GALATIANS 2:11–21

Is it possible that technological advances in communication have left us unable to confront people properly? After all, employers can now send layoff notices via e-mail. And people can criticize others on Facebook and Twitter instead of talking face to face. Perhaps it might be better to put all that aside and emulate how Paul communicated with Peter when they had a disagreement.

Paul had to confront Peter for compromising grace (Galatians 2:11–16). Peter had been fellowshiping with Gentiles, but when the Judaizers arrived (who believed that sinners are saved through Jesus plus keeping the law of Moses), Peter separated himself from the Gentiles. He ostracized them while professing to be one with them. Seeing this hypocrisy, Paul, in love and with passion, confronted Peter face to face for cowering to a legalistic system that was powerless to change lives. He vigorously reminded Peter that grace leads to freedom from sin's slavery and to obedience to God.

Having courageous conversations with fellow Christians can be difficult, but they will promote purity and unity. We can carry out our responsibility to one another to speak the truth in love (Ephesians 4:15) by walking in the power of the Holy Spirit.

———

A WELL-CHOSEN WORD
CAN SPEAK VOLUMES.

The LORD said to Moses, "Tell the Israelites to bring me an offering. You are to receive the offering for me from everyone whose heart prompts them to give. These are the offerings you are to receive from them: gold, silver and bronze; blue, purple and scarlet yarn and fine linen; goat hair; ram skins dyed red and another type of durable leather; acacia wood; olive oil for the light; spices for the anointing oil and for the fragrant incense; and onyx stones and other gems to be mounted on the ephod and breastpiece.

"Then have them make a sanctuary for me, and I will dwell among them. Make this tabernacle and all its furnishings exactly like the pattern I will show you."

EXODUS 25:1–9

A few years ago, my wife met a woman who needed a ride. She sensed that this could be from God, so she agreed to take her to her destination. During the ride, the woman revealed to my wife that she was a believer but she struggled with drug addiction. My wife listened to and talked with this hurting woman. As she gave her hope for a better tomorrow, I believe that in some small way the woman experienced a little piece of heaven on earth.

When God instructed Moses to build the tabernacle according to His specifications, it was so that God's people would sense His presence. I like to think of it as a little piece of heaven on earth. The temple was a physical example of God's presence on earth also (1 Kings 5–8). The purpose of these holy places was for God to dwell among His people. This was God's plan when Jesus, the perfect temple, "tabernacled" among us (John 1:14).

When Jesus ascended to heaven, He sent the Holy Spirit to indwell His followers (John 14:16–17), so we would be God's tabernacles and temples in the world (1 Corinthians 3:16; 6:19). As God's representatives of His presence, let's find ways to bring the peace and hope of heaven to others on earth.

———

A CHRISTIAN WHO IS WILLING TO DO
LITTLE THINGS FOR OTHERS CAN DO
GREAT THINGS FOR THE LORD.

Praise be to the God and Father of our Lord Jesus Christ, the Father of compassion and the God of all comfort, who comforts us in all our troubles, so that we can comfort those in any trouble with the comfort we ourselves receive from God. For just as we share abundantly in the sufferings of Christ, so also our comfort abounds through Christ. If we are distressed, it is for your comfort and salvation; if we are comforted, it is for your comfort, which produces in you patient endurance of the same sufferings we suffer. And our hope for you is firm, because we know that just as you share in our sufferings, so also you share in our comfort.

We do not want you to be uninformed, brothers and sisters, about the troubles we experienced in the province of Asia. We were under great pressure, far beyond our ability to endure, so that we despaired of life itself. Indeed, we felt we had received the sentence of death. But this happened that we might not rely on ourselves but on God, who raises the dead. He has delivered us from such a deadly peril, and he will deliver us again. On him we have set our hope that he will continue to deliver us, as you help us by your prayers. Then many will give thanks on our behalf for the gracious favor granted us in answer to the prayers of many.

2 CORINTHIANS 1:3–11

While speaking to a group of Christian athletes, I asked them how they normally responded to hardships. Their responses included fear, anger, self-pity, aggression, despair, abusive behavior, apathy, and turning to God. I encouraged them to trust that God would comfort them and then use them to comfort others.

Just as I encouraged those athletes, Paul encouraged a group of believers in a town called Corinth. He reminded them that afflictions were inevitable for the follower of Jesus. Many were being persecuted, imprisoned, and oppressed—all because of their relationship with Jesus. Paul wanted the Corinthians to know that in the midst of their trouble God was their source of help. He would come to their side and help them to have godly responses. Then Paul gave one of the reasons God allowed suffering and brought divine comfort—so the Corinthians might have the empathy to enter into other people's sorrow and comfort them (2 Corinthians 1:4).

When we suffer, let's remember this: God will bring comfort to us through His Word, by the Holy Spirit, and through fellow believers. God does not comfort us so we'll be comfortable; we are comforted by God so we might be comforters.

WHEN GOD PERMITS TRIALS,
HE ALSO PROVIDES COMFORT.

"And now, compelled by the Spirit, I am going to Jerusalem, not knowing what will happen to me there. I only know that in every city the Holy Spirit warns me that prison and hardships are facing me. However, I consider my life worth nothing to me; my only aim is to finish the race and complete the task the Lord Jesus has given me—the task of testifying to the good news of God's grace.

"Now I know that none of you among whom I have gone about preaching the kingdom will ever see me again. Therefore, I declare to you today that I am innocent of the blood of any of you. For I have not hesitated to proclaim to you the whole will of God. Keep watch over yourselves and all the flock of which the Holy Spirit has made you overseers. Be shepherds of the church of God, which he bought with his own blood. I know that after I leave, savage wolves will come in among you and will not spare the flock. Even from your own number men will arise and distort the truth in order to draw away disciples after them. So be on your guard! Remember that for three years I never stopped warning each of you night and day with tears.

"Now I commit you to God and to the word of his grace, which can build you up and give you an inheritance among all those who are sanctified."

ACTS 20:22–32

As my kids were discarding their trash at the local mall food court, my older son was almost run into by a man who was clearly on a mission. My younger son jokingly remarked, "Maybe he stole something." Thinking I might be able to use this as a teachable moment, I said, "That's what the Bible calls judging." He then asked with a smile: "Why are you always 'pastoring' me?" After I finished laughing, I told my sons that I could never take a vacation from shepherding them.

The apostle Paul told the Ephesian elders that they too could never take a vacation from shepherding God's people (Acts 20). He was convinced that false teachers would try to ravage the church (v. 29), and the elders needed to protect the group from them. Caring for God's people includes feeding them spiritually, leading them gently, and warning them firmly. Leaders in the church are to be motivated by the incalculable price Christ paid on the cross (v. 28).

Church leaders have a big responsibility to watch over our souls, for one day they will give an account to the Lord for their work among us. Let's bring them joy now by responding to their faithful, godly leadership with obedience and submission (Hebrews 13:17).

———

AFTER WE HEAR THE WORD OF GOD,
WE SHOULD THEN TAKE UP THE WORK OF GOD.

As Jesus walked beside the Sea of Galilee, he saw Simon and his brother Andrew casting a net into the lake, for they were fishermen. "Come, follow me," Jesus said, "and I will send you out to fish for people." At once they left their nets and followed him.

When he had gone a little farther, he saw James son of Zebedee and his brother John in a boat, preparing their nets. Without delay he called them, and they left their father Zebedee in the boat with the hired men and followed him.

MARK 1:16–20

I read about Captain Ray Baker, who flew for the Strategic Air Command during the Vietnam War. The Air Force trained him, along with the other pilots, to run out of their barracks to their planes at the sound of a buzzer. Many times during dinner he had to drop his utensils and bolt to his bomber. He had been trained to respond to the call with immediate obedience. He was so well-trained that one day while on furlough, he ran out of a restaurant when he heard a buzzer.

When Jesus called His first followers, they had an immediacy in their response to His call. The call of these fishermen was abrupt. Yet "at once they left their nets and followed him" (Mark 1:18). The author of this account, Mark, may have wanted to impress upon his readers the authority of Jesus. When He extended the call, these men jumped to obey because helping people enter the kingdom of God was a more compelling adventure and a grander vision than catching fish.

When Jesus issues a call to follow Him, He doesn't want us to delay. He expects immediate obedience when it comes to telling others the good news. Bring someone the story of salvation today!

———

WANTED: MESSENGERS TO DELIVER
THE GOOD NEWS.

Blessed is the one
  whose transgressions are forgiven,
  whose sins are covered.
Blessed is the one
  whose sin the LORD does not count against them
  and in whose spirit is no deceit.

When I kept silent,
  my bones wasted away
  through my groaning all day long.
For day and night
  your hand was heavy on me;
my strength was sapped
  as in the heat of summer.

Then I acknowledged my sin to you
  and did not cover up my iniquity.
I said, "I will confess
  my transgressions to the LORD."
And you forgave
  the guilt of my sin.

PSALM 32:1–5

For many years, Lake Okeechobee hid its secrets in thick waters and layers of muck. But when a drought shrank the Florida lake to its lowest level since officials began keeping records in 1932, hundreds of years of history was unveiled. Raking through the bottom of the lake, archaeologists found artifacts, pottery, boats, and even human bone fragments.

After King David committed adultery with Bathsheba and planned the death of her husband, Uriah, he covered his sins by denying them and not confessing them. He probably went many months conducting business as usual, even performing religious duties. As long as David cloaked his sinful secrets, he experienced God's crushing finger of conviction, and his strength evaporated like water in the heat of summer (Psalm 32:3–4).

When the prophet Nathan confronted David about his sin, God's conviction was so great that David confessed his sins to God and turned away from them. Immediately the Lord forgave David, and he experienced His mercy and grace (2 Samuel 12:13; Psalm 32:5; Psalm 51).

Let's be careful not to hide our sin. When we uncover our sins by confessing them to God, we are covered with His forgiveness.

———

GIVE GOD WHAT HE DESIRES MOST—
A BROKEN AND REPENTANT HEART.

"When you fast, do not look somber as the hypocrites do, for they disfigure their faces to show others they are fasting. Truly I tell you, they have received their reward in full. But when you fast, put oil on your head and wash your face, so that it will not be obvious to others that you are fasting, but only to your Father, who is unseen; and your Father, who sees what is done in secret, will reward you."

MATTHEW 6:16–18

A couple of years ago in our church we did a sermon series on the Old Testament tabernacle. Leading up to the message on the table of showbread, I did something I had never done before—I fasted from food for several days. I fasted because I wanted to experience the truth that "man does not live on bread alone but on every word that comes from the mouth of the LORD" (Deuteronomy 8:3). I wanted to deny myself something I love, food, for the God I love more. As I fasted, I followed Jesus's teaching about fasting in Matthew 6:16–18.

Jesus gave a negative command: "When you fast, do not look somber as hypocrites do" (v. 16). Then He gave a positive command about putting oil on your head and washing your face (v. 17). The two commands taken together meant that the people fasting should not draw attention to themselves. Jesus was teaching that this was a private act of sacrificial worship that should not provide any room for religious pride. Finally, He gave a promise: Your Father who sees what is done in secret will reward you (v. 18).

Although fasting isn't required, in giving up something we love, we may have a deeper experience of the God we love. He rewards us with himself.

———

MOVING AWAY FROM THE TABLE
CAN BRING US CLOSER TO THE FATHER.

*Jesus went up on a mountainside and called to him those
he wanted, and they came to him. He appointed twelve that
they might be with him and that he might send them out to
preach and to have authority to drive out demons. These are
the twelve he appointed: Simon (to whom he gave the name
Peter), James son of Zebedee and his brother John (to them
he gave the name Boanerges, which means "sons of thunder"),
Andrew, Philip, Bartholomew, Matthew, Thomas, James son
of Alphaeus, Thaddaeus, Simon the Zealot and Judas Iscariot,
who betrayed him.*

MARK 3:13–19

Because I am not a "fix it" kind of guy, I had to call a friend who is a great handyman to make some repairs in my home recently. He came over, and I gave him my list. But to my surprise, he told me I would be doing the repairs myself! He modeled for me how to do each job, instructed me along the way, and stayed with me. I followed his example and successfully made the repairs. This modeling seems close to what Jesus did when He called His first disciples.

When Jesus called those men to follow Him, He wanted them to be with Him and to teach the good news of the kingdom of God (Mark 1:14, 39; 6:12). The first job would require being under the immediate supervision of Jesus—learning His words and interpretation of the Scriptures and watching His behavior. For the second task, Jesus sent them out to preach (Mark 3:14–15)—saying what He said and doing what He did. As they carried out these tasks, they were to be dependent on Jesus.

Today, Jesus is still calling His followers to this simple, yet powerful process of discipleship—being with Him, following His instructions, and living His example. Are you dependent on Christ as you follow Him today?

———

DISCIPLESHIP IS RELATIONAL
AND EXPERIENTIAL.

"Even now," declares the LORD,
   "return to me with all your heart,
   with fasting and weeping and mourning."

Rend your heart
   and not your garments.
Return to the LORD *your God,*
   for he is gracious and compassionate,
slow to anger and abounding in love,
   and he relents from sending calamity.
Who knows? He may turn and relent
   and leave behind a blessing—
grain offerings and drink offerings
   for the LORD *your God.*

Blow the trumpet in Zion,
   declare a holy fast,
   call a sacred assembly.
Gather the people,
   consecrate the assembly; . . .
Let the priests, who minister before the LORD,
   weep between the portico and the altar.
Let them say, "Spare your people, LORD.
   Do not make your inheritance an object of scorn,
   a byword among the nations.
Why should they say among the peoples,
   'Where is their God?'"

JOEL 2:12–17

166

I didn't think the hesitation in my car engine and that little yellow "check engine" light on my dashboard really needed my immediate attention. I sang it away, saying I would get to it tomorrow. However, the next morning when I turned the key to start my car, it wouldn't start. My first reaction was frustration, knowing that this would mean money, time, and inconvenience. My second thought was more of a resolution: I need to pay attention to warning lights that are trying to get my attention. They can mean something is wrong.

In Joel 2:12–17, we read that God used the prophet Joel to encourage His people to pay attention to the warning light on their spiritual dashboard. Prosperity had caused them to become complacent and negligent in their commitment to the Lord. Their faith had degenerated into empty formalism and their lives into moral bankruptcy. So God sent a locust plague to ruin crops in order to get His people's attention (Joel 1), causing them to change their behavior and turn to Him with their whole heart.

What warning lights are flashing in your life? What needs to be tuned up or repaired through confession and repentance?

————

CONVICTION IS
GOD'S WARNING LIGHT.

If a malicious witness takes the stand to accuse someone of a crime, the two people involved in the dispute must stand in the presence of the LORD before the priests and the judges who are in office at the time. The judges must make a thorough investigation, and if the witness proves to be a liar, giving false testimony against a fellow Israelite, then do to the false witness as that witness intended to do to the other party. You must purge the evil from among you. The rest of the people will hear of this and be afraid, and never again will such an evil thing be done among you. Show no pity: life for life, eye for eye, tooth for tooth, hand for hand, foot for foot.

DEUTERONOMY 19:16–21; 5:38–45

One Sunday while preaching, a pastor was accosted and punched by a man. He continued preaching, and the man was arrested. The pastor prayed for him and even visited him in jail a few days later. What an example of the way to respond to insult and injury!

While there is a place for self-defense, personal revenge was forbidden in the Old Testament: "Do not seek revenge or bear a grudge against anyone among your people, but love your neighbor as yourself" (Leviticus 19:18; see also Deuteronomy 32:35). It was also forbidden by Jesus and the apostles (Matthew 5:38–45; Romans 12:17; 1 Peter 3:9).

The Old Testament law exacted like for like (Exodus 21:23–25; Deuteronomy 19:21), which ensured that judicial punishment was not unjust or malicious. But there was a larger principle looming when it came to personal revenge: Justice must be done, but it must be left in the hands of God or the authorities ordained by God.

Instead of returning injury and insult, may we live by Christ-honoring and Spirit-empowered alternatives: Live at peace with everyone (Romans 12:18), submit to a spiritual mediator (1 Corinthians 6:1–6), and leave it in the hands of authorities and, most of all, in God's hands.

———

LEAVE FINAL JUSTICE
IN THE HANDS OF A JUST GOD.

Do not steal.
Do not lie.
Do not deceive one another.
Do not swear falsely by my name and so profane the name
of your God. I am the LORD.
Do not defraud or rob your neighbor.
Do not hold back the wages of a hired worker overnight.
Do not curse the deaf or put a stumbling block in front of
the blind, but fear your God. I am the LORD.
Do not pervert justice; do not show partiality to the poor
or favoritism to the great, but judge your neighbor fairly.
Do not go about spreading slander among your people.
Do not do anything that endangers your neighbor's life.
I am the LORD.
Do not hate a fellow Israelite in your heart. Rebuke your
neighbor frankly so you will not share in their guilt.
Do not seek revenge or bear a grudge against anyone
among your people, but love your neighbor as yourself.
I am the LORD.

LEVITICUS 19:11–18

In 1955, when the US South was still highly segregated, Emmett Till, a black teenager from Chicago, visited relatives in Mississippi. After Emmett "dared" to talk to a white woman, two white men brutally murdered him. An all-white, male jury found the two "not guilty"—after deliberating for barely an hour. The two men later confessed to the crime in a *Life* magazine article.

Following the verdict, Emmett's mother said, "Two months ago I had a nice apartment in Chicago. I had a good job. I had a son. When something happened to Negroes in the South, I said, 'That's their business, not mine.' Now I know how wrong I was. The murder of my son has shown me that what happens to any of us, anywhere in the world, had better be the business of us all."

Making another's concerns our own is what Leviticus 19:18 calls us to do: "Love your neighbor as yourself." Jesus quotes this verse and interprets it as not placing any limitations on loving those around us (Matthew 22:39; Luke 10:25–37). Our neighbor doesn't just mean someone close by; it's anyone who has a need. We are to care for others as we care for ourselves.

To love our neighbor means to make the persecution, suffering, and injustice of our fellow human beings our own. It is the business of all who follow Christ.

———

COMPASSION PUTS LOVE
INTO ACTION.

*One of the criminals who hung there hurled insults at him:
"Aren't you the Messiah? Save yourself and us!"*

*But the other criminal rebuked him. "Don't you fear God,"
he said, "since you are under the same sentence? We are
punished justly, for we are getting what our deeds deserve.
But this man has done nothing wrong."*

*Then he said, "Jesus, remember me when you come into
your kingdom."*

*Jesus answered him, "Truly I tell you, today you will be
with me in paradise."*

LUKE 23:39–43

Pastor and author Erwin Lutzer wrote: "One minute after you slip behind the parted curtain, you will either be enjoying a personal welcome from Christ or catching your first glimpse of gloom as you have never known it. Either way, your future will be irrevocably fixed and eternally unchangeable."

Luke recorded a short yet powerful narrative that pictures two men about to go behind that curtain of death. When Jesus was being crucified, two thieves hung alongside Him. According to Mark, both men hurled insults at Jesus (15:32).

One of the thieves, however, had a change of heart as he realized Jesus's innocence, his own sin, and his destiny. He rebuked the other thief and asked Jesus to remember him when He came into His kingdom. These words were a sign of repentance and simple faith. Jesus responded, "Truly, I tell you, today you will be with me in paradise" (Luke 23:43). Salvation for the man was immediate. He knew that day where he would spend eternity.

Realizing that we are sinners and placing our trust in Jesus's death and resurrection assures us that we can immediately know where we will spend our eternal tomorrows when we slip behind the parted curtain.

———

TO PREPARE FOR TOMORROW,
TRUST JESUS TODAY.

But godliness with contentment is great gain. For we brought nothing into the world, and we can take nothing out of it. But if we have food and clothing, we will be content with that. Those who want to get rich fall into temptation and a trap and into many foolish and harmful desires that plunge people into ruin and destruction. For the love of money is a root of all kinds of evil. Some people, eager for money, have wandered from the faith and pierced themselves with many griefs.

1 TIMOTHY 6:6–10

An online survey conducted by a New York law firm revealed that 52 percent of Wall Street traders, brokers, investment bankers, and other financial service professionals have either engaged in illegal activity or believe they may need to do so in order to be successful. The survey concludes that these financial leaders "have lost their moral compass" and "accept corporate wrongdoing as a necessary evil."

In mentoring young Timothy, the apostle Paul warned that the love of money and the desire to get rich had caused some to lose their way. They had yielded to temptations and embraced many "foolish and harmful" desires (1 Timothy 6:9). Paul saw "the love of money" (not money itself) as a source of "all kinds of evil" (v. 10), especially the evil of trusting in money rather than depending on Christ.

As we learn to see that Jesus is the source of all we have, we will find contentment in Him rather than in material possessions. When we seek godliness rather than riches, we will gain a desire to be faithful with what we have been given.

Let's deliberately cultivate an attitude of contentment in God and faithfully submit to Him, for our Provider will care for us.

———

TO LOVE MONEY IS TO LOSE SIGHT
OF THE SOURCE OF LIFE.

Praise be to the God and Father of our Lord Jesus Christ, who has blessed us in the heavenly realms with every spiritual blessing in Christ. For he chose us in him before the creation of the world to be holy and blameless in his sight. In love he predestined us for adoption to sonship through Jesus Christ, in accordance with his pleasure and will—to the praise of his glorious grace, which he has freely given us in the One he loves. In him we have redemption through his blood, the forgiveness of sins, in accordance with the riches of God's grace that he lavished on us. With all wisdom and understanding, he made known to us the mystery of his will according to his good pleasure, which he purposed in Christ, to be put into effect when the times reach their fulfillment—to bring unity to all things in heaven and on earth under Christ.

In him we were also chosen, having been predestined according to the plan of him who works out everything in conformity with the purpose of his will, in order that we, who were the first to put our hope in Christ, might be for the praise of his glory. And you also were included in Christ when you heard the message of truth, the gospel of your salvation. When you believed, you were marked in him with a seal, the promised Holy Spirit, who is a deposit guaranteeing our inheritance until the redemption of those who are God's possession—to the praise of his glory.

EPHESIANS 1:3–14

There are some things money can't buy—but these days, not many," according to Michael Sandel, author of *What Money Can't Buy*. A person can buy a prison-cell upgrade for $90 a night, the right to shoot an endangered black rhino for $250,000, and your doctor's cell phone number for $1,500. It seems that "almost everything is up for sale."

But one thing money can't buy is *redemption*—freedom from the stranglehold of sin. When the apostle Paul began writing about the rich nature of God's plan of salvation through Jesus, his heart erupted in praise: "In him we have redemption through his blood, the forgiveness of sins, in accordance with the riches of God's grace that he lavished on us" (Ephesians 1:7–8).

Jesus's death on the cross was the high cost of delivering us from sin. And only He could pay that price because He was the perfect Son of God. The natural response to such free but costly grace is spontaneous praise from our hearts and commitment to the God who bought us through Jesus (1:13–14).

Praise to our loving God—He has come to set us free!

———

ONLY JESUS'S DEATH COULD
PURCHASE OUR FREEDOM.

*Listen to my words, L*ORD*, consider my lament.*
   Hear my cry for help, my King and my God, for to you I pray.

*In the morning, L*ORD*, you hear my voice;*
   in the morning I lay my requests before you and wait expectantly.
For you are not a God who is pleased with wickedness;
   with you, evil people are not welcome.
The arrogant cannot stand in your presence.
   You hate all who do wrong; you destroy those who tell lies.
*The bloodthirsty and deceitful you, L*ORD*, detest.*
   But I, by your great love, can come into your house;
in reverence I bow down toward your holy temple.

*Lead me, L*ORD*, in your righteousness because of my enemies—*
   make your way straight before me.
Not a word from their mouth can be trusted;
   their heart is filled with malice.
Their throat is an open grave; with their tongues they tell lies.
Declare them guilty, O God!
   Let their intrigues be their downfall.
Banish them for their many sins, for they have rebelled against you.
But let all who take refuge in you be glad; let them ever sing for joy.
Spread your protection over them,
   that those who love your name may rejoice in you.

*Surely, L*ORD*, you bless the righteous;*
   you surround them with your favor as with a shield.

PSALM 5

The day before Billy Graham's 1982 interview on NBC's *Today Show*, his director of public relations, Larry Ross, requested a private room for Graham to pray in before the interview. But when Mr. Graham arrived at the studio, his assistant informed Ross that Mr. Graham didn't need the room. He said, "Mr. Graham started praying when he got up this morning, he prayed while eating breakfast, he prayed on the way over in the car, and he'll probably be praying all the way through the interview." Ross later said, "That was a great lesson for me to learn as a young man."

Prayerfulness is not an event; it is a way of being in relationship with God. This kind of intimate relationship is developed when God's people view prayerfulness as a way of life. The Psalms encourage us to begin each day by lifting our voice to the Lord (Psalm 5:3); to fill our day with conversations with God (55:17); and in the face of accusations and slander, to give ourselves totally to prayer (109:4). We develop prayer as a way of life because we desire to be with God (42:1–4; 84:1–2; 130:5–6).

Prayer is our way of connecting with God in all of life's circumstances. God is always listening. We can—and should—talk to Him throughout the day.

———

IN PRAYER,
GOD HEARS MORE THAN YOUR WORDS—
HE LISTENS TO YOUR HEART.

That day when evening came, he said to his disciples, "Let us go over to the other side." Leaving the crowd behind, they took him along, just as he was, in the boat. There were also other boats with him. A furious squall came up, and the waves broke over the boat, so that it was nearly swamped. Jesus was in the stern, sleeping on a cushion. The disciples woke him and said to him, "Teacher, don't you care if we drown?"

He got up, rebuked the wind and said to the waves, "Quiet! Be still!" Then the wind died down and it was completely calm.

He said to his disciples, "Why are you so afraid? Do you still have no faith?"

They were terrified and asked each other, "Who is this? Even the wind and the waves obey him!"

MARK 4:35–41

While Hurricane Katrina headed toward the coast of Mississippi, a retired pastor and his wife left their home and went to a shelter. Their daughter pleaded with them to go to Atlanta where she could take care of them, but the couple couldn't get any money to make the trip because the banks were closed. After the storm had passed, they returned to their home to get a few belongings and were able to salvage only a few family photos floating in the water. Then, when the man was taking his father's photo out of its frame so it could dry, $366 fell out—precisely the amount needed for two plane tickets to Atlanta. They learned they could trust Jesus for what they needed.

For the disciples, trusting Jesus in a storm was the curriculum for the day in the dramatic narrative of Mark 4:35–41. Jesus had instructed His disciples to cross to the other side of the Sea of Galilee, and then He went to sleep in the boat. When a quick and violent storm blew in, the disciples dripped as much with fear and anxiety as water from the waves. They woke Jesus, saying, "Teacher, don't you care if we drown?" (v. 38). Jesus stood up and with three words, "Quiet! Be still!" He muzzled the storm.

We all experience storms—persecutions, financial troubles, illnesses, disappointments, loneliness—and Jesus does not always prevent them. But He has promised never to leave us nor forsake us (Hebrews 13:5). He will keep us calm in the storm.

———

IN THE STORMS OF LIFE,
WE CAN SEE THE CHARACTER OF OUR GOD.

When God made his promise to Abraham, since there was
no one greater for him to swear by, he swore by himself, saying,
"I will surely bless you and give you many descendants."
And so after waiting patiently, Abraham received what was
promised.

People swear by someone greater than themselves, and the
oath confirms what is said and puts an end to all argument.
Because God wanted to make the unchanging nature of
his purpose very clear to the heirs of what was promised,
he confirmed it with an oath. God did this so that, by two
unchangeable things in which it is impossible for God to lie,
we who have fled to take hold of the hope set before us may be
greatly encouraged. We have this hope as an anchor for the
soul, firm and secure. It enters the inner sanctuary behind
the curtain, where our forerunner, Jesus, has entered on our
behalf. He has become a high priest forever, in the order of
Melchizedek.

HEBREWS 6:13–20

After Estella Pyfrom retired from teaching, she bought a bus, decked it out with computers and desks, and now drives the "Brilliant Bus" through Palm Beach County, Florida, providing a place for at-risk children to do their homework and learn technology. Estella is providing stability and hope to children who might be tempted to throw away their dream for a better tomorrow.

In the first century, an avalanche of suffering and discouragement threatened the Christian community. The author of Hebrews wrote to convince these followers of Christ not to throw away their confidence in their future hope (2:1). Their hope—a faith in God for salvation and entrance into heaven—was found in the person and sacrifice of Christ. When Jesus entered heaven after His resurrection, He secured their hope for the future (6:19–20). Like an anchor dropped at sea, preventing a ship from drifting away, Jesus's death, resurrection, and return to heaven brought assurance and stability to the believers' lives. This hope for the future cannot and will not be shaken loose.

Because Jesus anchors our souls, we will not drift away from our hope in God.

OUR HOPE IS ANCHORED IN JESUS.

Praise be to the God and Father of our Lord Jesus Christ, who has blessed us in the heavenly realms with every spiritual blessing in Christ. For he chose us in him before the creation of the world to be holy and blameless in his sight. In love he predestined us for adoption to sonship through Jesus Christ, in accordance with his pleasure and will—to the praise of his glorious grace, which he has freely given us in the One he loves. In him we have redemption through his blood, the forgiveness of sins, in accordance with the riches of God's grace that he lavished on us. With all wisdom and understanding, he made known to us the mystery of his will according to his good pleasure, which he purposed in Christ, to be put into effect when the times reach their fulfillment—to bring unity to all things in heaven and on earth under Christ.

In him we were also chosen, having been predestined according to the plan of him who works out everything in conformity with the purpose of his will, in order that we, who were the first to put our hope in Christ, might be for the praise of his glory. And you also were included in Christ when you heard the message of truth, the gospel of your salvation. When you believed, you were marked in him with a seal, the promised Holy Spirit, who is a deposit guaranteeing our inheritance until the redemption of those who are God's possession—to the praise of his glory.

EPHESIANS 1:3–14

In 2005, when American civil rights hero Rosa Parks died, Oprah Winfrey counted it a privilege to eulogize her. Oprah said of the woman who refused to give up her bus seat to a white man in 1955, "I often thought about what that took—knowing the climate of the times and what could have happened to you—what it took to stay seated. You acted without concern for yourself and made life better for us all."

We often use the word *eulogy* to refer to the words spoken at a funeral. But it can also refer to other situations where we give high praise to someone. In the opening lines of Ephesians, the apostle Paul eulogized the living God. When he said, "Praise be to the God and Father," he used a word for "praise" that means "eulogy." Paul invited the Ephesians to join him in praising God for all kinds of spiritual blessings: God had chosen and adopted them; Jesus had redeemed, forgiven, and made known to them the mystery of the gospel; and the Spirit had guaranteed and sealed them. This great salvation was purely an act of God and His grace.

Let us continue to center our thoughts on God's blessings in Christ. When we do, like Paul, we will find our hearts overflowing with a eulogy that declares: "To the praise of His glory."

PRAISE IS THE SONG
OF A SOUL SET FREE.

An unfriendly person pursues selfish ends
* and against all sound judgment starts quarrels.*
Fools find no pleasure in understanding
* but delight in airing their own opinions.*
When wickedness comes, so does contempt,
* and with shame comes reproach.*
The words of the mouth are deep waters,
* but the fountain of wisdom is a rushing stream.*
It is not good to be partial to the wicked
* and so deprive the innocent of justice.*
The lips of fools bring them strife,
* and their mouths invite a beating.*
The mouths of fools are their undoing,
* and their lips are a snare to their very lives.*
The words of a gossip are like choice morsels;
* they go down to the inmost parts…*

From the fruit of their mouth a person's stomach is filled;
* with the harvest of their lips they are satisfied.*
The tongue has the power of life and death,
* and those who love it will eat its fruit.*

                                    PROVERBS 18:1–8; 20–21

Nelson Mandela, who opposed the South African apartheid regime and was imprisoned for almost three decades, knew the power of words. He is often quoted today, but while in prison his words could not be quoted for fear of repercussion. A decade after his release he said: "It is never my custom to use words lightly. If twenty-seven years in prison have done anything to us, it was to use the silence of solitude to make us understand how precious words are, and how real speech is in its impact on the way people live and die."

King Solomon, author of most of the Old Testament book of Proverbs, wrote often about the power of words. He said, "The tongue has the power of life and death" (Proverbs 18:21). Words have the potential to produce positive or negative consequences (v. 20). They have the power to give life through encouragement and honesty or to crush and kill through lies and gossip. How can we be assured of producing good words that have a positive outcome? The only way is by diligently guarding our hearts: "Above all else, guard your heart, for everything you do flows from it" (4:23).

Jesus can transform our hearts so that our words can truly be their best—honest, calm, appropriate, and suitable for the situation.

OUR WORDS HAVE THE POWER
TO BUILD UP OR TEAR DOWN.

Your word is a lamp for my feet,
a light on my path.
I have taken an oath and confirmed it,
that I will follow your righteous laws.
I have suffered much;
*preserve my life, L*ORD*, according to your word.*
*Accept, L*ORD*, the willing praise of my mouth,*
and teach me your laws.
Though I constantly take my life in my hands,
I will not forget your law.
The wicked have set a snare for me,
but I have not strayed from your precepts.
Your statutes are my heritage forever;
they are the joy of my heart.
My heart is set on keeping your decrees
to the very end.

PSALM 119:105–112

During World War II, small compasses saved the lives of twenty-seven sailors three hundred miles off the coast of North Carolina. Waldemar Semenov, a retired merchant seaman, was serving as a junior engineer aboard the SS *Alcoa Guide* when a German submarine surfaced and opened fire on the ship. The ship was hit, caught fire, and began to sink. Semenov and his crew lowered compass-equipped lifeboats into the water and used the compasses to guide them toward the shipping lanes closer to shore. After three days, the men were rescued.

The psalmist reminded God's people that His Word was a trustworthy "compass." He likened it to a lamp. In that day, the flickering light cast by an olive oil lamp was only bright enough to show a traveler his next step. To the psalmist, God's Word was such a lamp, providing enough light to illuminate the path for those pursuing God (Psalm 119:105). When the psalmist was wandering in the dark on a chaotic path of life, he believed that God, through the guidance of His Word, would provide direction.

When we lose our bearings in life, we can trust our God. He gives His trustworthy Word as our compass, using it to lead us into deeper fellowship with Him.

———

GOD HAS GIVEN US HIS WORD
TO HELP US KNOW AND FOLLOW HIM.

When the woman saw that the fruit of the tree was good for food and pleasing to the eye, and also desirable for gaining wisdom, she took some and ate it. She also gave some to her husband, who was with her, and he ate it. Then the eyes of both of them were opened, and they realized they were naked; so they sewed fig leaves together and made coverings for themselves.

Then the man and his wife heard the sound of the Lord God as he was walking in the garden in the cool of the day, and they hid from the Lord God among the trees of the garden. But the Lord God called to the man, "Where are you?"

He answered, "I heard you in the garden, and I was afraid because I was naked; so I hid."

And he said, "Who told you that you were naked? Have you eaten from the tree that I commanded you not to eat from?"

The man said, "The woman you put here with me—she gave me some fruit from the tree, and I ate it."

Then the Lord God said to the woman, "What is this you have done?"

The woman said, "The serpent deceived me, and I ate." ...

And the Lord God said, "The man has now become like one of us, knowing good and evil. He must not be allowed to reach out his hand and take also from the tree of life and eat, and live forever." So the Lord God banished him from the Garden of Eden to work the ground from which he had been taken.

GENESIS 3:6–13, 22–23

In August 2013, large crowds gathered at the Phipps Conservatory in Pittsburgh, Pennsylvania, to witness the blooming of the tropical plant known as the corpse flower. Since the flower is native to Indonesia and may flower only once every several years, its blooming is a spectacle. Once open, the huge spiky, beautiful, red bloom smells like rotten meat. Because of its putrid fragrance, the flower attracts flies and beetles that are looking for rotting meat. But there is no nectar.

Like the corpse flower, sin holds out promises but in the end offers no rewards. Adam and Eve found this out the hard way. Eden was beautiful until they ruined it by doing the one thing God urged them not to do. Tempted to doubt God's goodness, they ignored their Creator's loving warning and soon lost their innocence. The God-given beauty of the tree of the knowledge of good and evil became like a corpse flower to them. The reward for their disobedience was alienation, pain, emptiness, toil, and death.

Sin looks inviting and may feel good, but it doesn't compare with the wonder, beauty, and fragrance of trusting and obeying God, who has made us to share His life and joy.

———

GOD'S COMMANDS CAN OVERPOWER
SATAN'S SUGGESTIONS.

Praise the Lord.

Praise God in his sanctuary;
*   praise him in his mighty heavens.*
Praise him for his acts of power;
*   praise him for his surpassing greatness.*
Praise him with the sounding of the trumpet,
*   praise him with the harp and lyre,*
praise him with timbrel and dancing,
*   praise him with the strings and pipe,*
praise him with the clash of cymbals,
*   praise him with resounding cymbals.*

Let everything that has breath praise the Lord.

Praise the Lord.

PSALM 150

After Ghana's Asamoah Gyan scored a goal against Germany in the 2014 World Cup, he and his teammates did a coordinated dance step. When Germany's Miroslav Klose scored a few minutes later, he did a running front flip. "Soccer celebrations are so appealing because they reveal players' personalities, values, and passions," says Clint Mathis, who scored for the US at the 2002 World Cup.

In Psalm 150, the psalmist invites "everything that has breath" to celebrate and praise the Lord in many different ways. He suggests that we use trumpets and harps, stringed instruments and pipes, cymbals and dancing. He encourages us to creatively and passionately celebrate, honor, and adore the Lord. Because the Lord is great and has performed mighty acts on behalf of His people, He is worthy of all praise. These outward expressions of praise will come from an inner wellspring overflowing with gratitude to God. "Let everything that has breath praise the Lord," the psalmist declares (150:6).

Though we may celebrate the Lord in different ways (I'm not encouraging back flips in our worship services), our praise to God always needs to be expressive and meaningful. When we think about the Lord's character and His mighty acts toward us, we cannot help but celebrate Him through our praise and worship.

EACH NEW DAY
GIVES US NEW REASONS
TO SING GOD'S PRAISE.

In that day you will say:

> "*I will praise you, Lord.*
> *Although you were angry with me,*
> *your anger has turned away*
> *and you have comforted me.*
> *Surely God is my salvation;*
> *I will trust and not be afraid.*
> *The Lord, the Lord himself, is my strength and my defense;*
> *he has become my salvation.*"
> *With joy you will draw water*
> *from the wells of salvation.*

In that day you will say:

> "*Give praise to the Lord, proclaim his name;*
> *make known among the nations what he has done,*
> *and proclaim that his name is exalted.*
> *Sing to the Lord, for he has done glorious things;*
> *let this be known to all the world.*
> *Shout aloud and sing for joy, people of Zion,*
> *for great is the Holy One of Israel among you.*"

ISAIAH 12

When people drill holes deep into the earth, it is normally for pulling up core samples of rock, accessing oil, or finding water.

In Isaiah 12, we learn that God wanted His people, who were living in a spiritual desert as well as a geographical desert, to discover His "wells of salvation." The prophet Isaiah compared God's salvation to a well from which the most refreshing of all waters can be drawn. After many years of turning their back on God, the nation of Judah was destined for exile as God allowed foreign invaders to conquer the nation, scattering the people. Yet, said the prophet Isaiah, a remnant would eventually return to their homeland as a sign that God was with them (Isaiah 11:11–12).

Isaiah 12 is a hymn, praising God for His faithfulness in keeping His promises, especially the promise of salvation. Isaiah encouraged the people that deep in God's "wells of salvation" they would experience the cool water of God's grace, strength, and joy (vv. 1–3). This would refresh and strengthen their hearts and cause praise and gratitude to God (vv. 4–6).

God wants each of us to discover—through confession and repentance—the deep, cool waters of joy found in the everlasting wells of His salvation.

———

THE WELLS OF GOD'S SALVATION
NEVER RUN DRY.

Leaving that place, Jesus withdrew to the region of Tyre and Sidon. A Canaanite woman from that vicinity came to him, crying out, "Lord, Son of David, have mercy on me! My daughter is demon-possessed and suffering terribly."

Jesus did not answer a word. So his disciples came to him and urged him, "Send her away, for she keeps crying out after us."

He answered, "I was sent only to the lost sheep of Israel."

The woman came and knelt before him. "Lord, help me!" she said.

He replied, "It is not right to take the children's bread and toss it to the dogs."

"Yes it is, Lord," she said. "Even the dogs eat the crumbs that fall from their master's table."

Then Jesus said to her, "Woman, you have great faith! Your request is granted." And her daughter was healed at that moment.

MATTHEW 15:21–28

In 1953, a fledgling business called Rocket Chemical Company and its staff of three set out to create a line of rust-prevention solvents and degreasers for use in the aerospace industry. It took them forty attempts to perfect their formula. The original secret formula for WD-40—which stands for Water Displacement, 40th attempt—is still in use today. In a recent year, WD-40 had sales of more than $380 million. What a story of persistence!

The gospel of Matthew records another story of bold persistence. A Canaanite woman had a daughter who was possessed by a demon. She had no hope for her daughter—until she heard that Jesus was in the region.

This desperate woman came to Jesus with her need because she believed He could help her. She cried out to Him even though everything and everybody seemed to be against her—race, religious background, gender, the disciples, Satan, and seemingly even Jesus (Matthew 15:22–27). Despite all of these obstacles, she did not give up. With bold persistence, she pushed her way through the dark corridors of difficulty, desperate need, and rejection. The result? Jesus commended her for her faith and healed her daughter (v. 28).

We too are invited to approach Jesus with bold persistence. As we keep asking, seeking, and knocking, we will find grace and mercy in our time of need.

PERSISTENCE IN PRAYER
PLEASES GOD.

Now the serpent was more crafty than any of the wild animals the Lord God had made. He said to the woman, "Did God really say, 'You must not eat from any tree in the garden'?"

The woman said to the serpent, "We may eat fruit from the trees in the garden, but God did say, 'You must not eat fruit from the tree that is in the middle of the garden, and you must not touch it, or you will die.'"

"You will not certainly die," the serpent said to the woman. "For God knows that when you eat from it your eyes will be opened, and you will be like God, knowing good and evil."

When the woman saw that the fruit of the tree was good for food and pleasing to the eye, and also desirable for gaining wisdom, she took some and ate it. She also gave some to her husband, who was with her, and he ate it. Then the eyes of both of them were opened, and they realized they were naked; so they sewed fig leaves together and made coverings for themselves.

Then the man and his wife heard the sound of the Lord God as he was walking in the garden in the cool of the day, and they hid from the Lord God among the trees of the garden. But the Lord God called to the man, "Where are you?"

He answered, "I heard you in the garden, and I was afraid because I was naked; so I hid."

And he said, "Who told you that you were naked? Have you eaten from the tree that I commanded you not to eat from?"

The man said, "The woman you put here with me—she gave me some fruit from the tree, and I ate it."

Then the Lord God said to the woman, "What is this you have done?"

The woman said, "The serpent deceived me, and I ate."

GENESIS 3:1–13

A city employee in Lodi, California, sued the city for damages after he backed a dump truck into his own parked car. The 51-year-old man argued that because the "city's vehicle damaged my private vehicle," the city owed him $3,600. As ridiculous as this sounds, blaming others has been a basic human trait since the beginning.

When Adam and Eve ate from the forbidden tree, their eyes were opened and they lost their innocence. God asked the man a simple, yet penetrating question: "Where are you?" (Genesis 3:9). In the past, Adam had intimate fellowship with God, but now he responded in fear and hid himself.

God's follow-up question was more convicting than the first: "Have you eaten from the tree that I commanded you not to eat from?" (v. 11). Then the blame game started: "The woman you put here with me—she gave me some fruit from the tree, and I ate it" (v. 12). The man blamed God and the woman for his sin. The woman blamed the serpent rather than herself. Ever since that day in the garden of Eden, we tend to blame others rather than ourselves for our sinful choices.

When we sin, we should take responsibility. Let's pray like David: "I acknowledged my sin to you and did not cover up my iniquity" (Psalm 32:5).

THE FIRST STEP IN REPENTING FROM SIN
IS TO ADMIT THAT YOU ARE TO BLAME.

Now Peter was sitting out in the courtyard, and a servant girl came to him. "You also were with Jesus of Galilee," she said.

But he denied it before them all. "I don't know what you're talking about," he said.

Then he went out to the gateway, where another servant girl saw him and said to the people there, "This fellow was with Jesus of Nazareth."

He denied it again, with an oath: "I don't know the man!"

After a little while, those standing there went up to Peter and said, "Surely you are one of them; your accent gives you away."

Then he began to call down curses, and he swore to them, "I don't know the man!"

Immediately a rooster crowed. Then Peter remembered the word Jesus had spoken: "Before the rooster crows, you will disown me three times." And he went outside and wept bitterly.

MATTHEW 26:69–75

According to psychologist Perry Buffington, failure takes on a life of its own because the brain remembers incomplete tasks or failures longer than successes or completed activities. It's called the "Zeigarnik effect." Buffington states, "When a project or a thought is completed, the brain … no longer gives the project priority or active working status…. But failures have no closure. The brain continues to spin the memory, trying to come up with ways to fix the mess and move it from active to inactive status."

Peter failed in many ways, but Jesus fixed the mounting mess of the apostle's failures and moved his blunders from active to inactive status. He failed because the deluge of his pride overpowered him, and he attempted to blanket himself in his own strength. At the arrest of Jesus, he collapsed and became a coward (Matthew 26:69–75). His heart deceived him and he denied his Lord. But Jesus gave him a second chance and moved his failure from active to inactive (Mark 16:7; John 21:15–17).

Jesus can move our failure to inactive status when we realize that He's bigger than our failures and He's willing to give us another chance. If our failures are the result of sin, we should confess our sins to God and genuinely repent (1 John 1:9). When we fail, we can and should get up again (Proverbs 24:16). And we should press on in Jesus's power (Acts 3).

―――

SUCCESS OFTEN RISES OUT
OF THE ASHES OF FAILURE.

"This, then, is how you should pray:

"'Our Father in heaven,
hallowed be your name,
your kingdom come,
your will be done,
    on earth as it is in heaven.
Give us today our daily bread.
And forgive us our debts,
    as we also have forgiven our debtors.
And lead us not into temptation,
    but deliver us from the evil one.'"

MATTHEW 6:9–13

Not long ago, I traveled to the Democratic Republic of Congo to lead a Bible conference. I took in the beauty of the Nyungwe Forest and Ruzizi River, which separates Congo from Rwanda. I experienced the amazing hospitality of the Congolese people, and I was moved by their sincere faith in God's provision.

Because unemployment, poverty, and malnutrition are serious problems there, the people often don't know where their next meal will come from. So each time they sit down to eat, they thank God and ask Him to provide the next meal.

Their prayer sounds a lot like Jesus's prayer in Matthew 6:11, "Give us today our daily bread." The word *bread* refers to any food. The word *today* indicates provision that came to them one day at a time.

Many first-century workers were paid one day at a time, so a few days' illness could spell tragedy. *Daily* could be translated "for the coming day." The prayer would read: "Give us today our bread for the coming day." It was an urgent prayer to those who lived from hand to mouth.

This prayer calls Jesus's followers everywhere to recognize that our ability to work and earn our food comes from God's hand.

———

OUR PROBLEMS ARE NEVER A STRAIN
ON GOD'S PROVISION.

Note to the Reader

The publisher invites you to share your response to the message of this book by writing Discovery House, P.O. Box 3566, Grand Rapids, MI 49501, U.S.A. For information about other Discovery House books, music, or DVDs, contact us at the same address or call 1-800-653-8333. Find us online at dhp.org or send e-mail to books@dhp.org.